A LIFETIME BEHIND BARS

A LIFETIME BEHIND BARS

COLIN FISHER
Illustrations by Marzena Terry

A Lifetime Behind Bars

A brief glimpse behind the scenes of when a naïve, but determined, young couple decided to take on a dilapidated country pub in the heart of Wiltshire, England and turned it into a hugely successful catering establishment.

To people contemplating the trade, those already committed, and to anyone just curious.

Colin and Kate Fisher

A Life Behind Bars

PREFACE

When you operate a country public house, or a community public house, it is a challenging experience. You become intrinsically involved in almost everything that is happening in the vicinity. Personal relationships, problems, events, local disputes and other issues are all openly discussed in your presence. You are required to become a very good listener, but take great care not to take sides or voice your own opinions even if you would dearly like to! Certain subjects, mentioned later, are best avoided. You also meet customers from all walks of life, from the locals in very menial jobs, to Lords and Ladies, sometimes all in the same day.

There was a Public bar at The Royal Oak which was used predominantly by locals from the village and regulars from the region. The small Lounge bar was used by the gentry and a few locals who did not wish to mingle with other villagers for various reasons! This amazing mixture of people and their behavior, resulted in a bounty of interesting experiences.

In many ways, to be successful, operating a busy bar is like being on stage. Regardless of what is going on behind the scenes, personal issues or disputes must be disregarded and you walk out on stage to greet your customers with a welcoming smile. This is easier said than done and later experiences when visiting pubs in all parts of the country convinced me that quite a few licensees were in the wrong job! After many years of operating a country pub and witnessing an incredible number of memorable events, I would like to share just a few with you.

PART ONE

Part One is targeted at those folk considering the trade, those already in the trade and those just wanting an informative glimpse of pub life behind the scenes and of course anyone still alive who may be mentioned. This is not. a biography but some memories we wish to share.

All of the stories are true. However, I have changed names and dates in places. Without the following, none of the events described would have occurred; Kate, my wife, Chef and backbone of the business; the bar staff (the best in the area); the kitchen staff (most of them very talented); the local characters.

PART TWO

The final section is not designed as a reference of how the industry developed, but is our interpretation of how the pub sector was hugely manipulated in the late 1980's. The people connected with Part Two are comprised of; dear friends involved in the Pub's; Graham, John and other partners at Moore Stephens Chartered Accountants and Milestone accountants; the wonderful teams in the regional offices and also in Mumbai. Also, challenging working relationships with senior management in most major Pub Companies!

THE BEGINNING

Two years married, a three month old son, a new bungalow, a mortgage and a really good job (with prospects). A pessimist would say,

"Hardly the time to throw caution to the wind and take on a country pub!"

But that is exactly what we did!

It was 1967. I had completed a short service commission in the Royal Navy as a pilot and then worked my way up to become the sales manager at Downton Engineering works, located near Salisbury, Wiltshire. Kate, now aged twenty, had been a nurse at St. Bartholomew's hospital when we met. I was aged twenty-three and with Kate, had a combined business experience of sweet F.A.!

In 1967, "The Royal Oak Inn", a Public House, situated in Great Wishford, near Salisbury, was owned by Ushers Brewery of Trowbridge, Wiltshire. Great Wishford is a picturesque village, in the heart of Wiltshire, about six miles from the beautiful Cathedral city of Salisbury. The main road into the village crosses a bridge over the River Wyle and then winds through stone walled old streets to the village itself. In the center of the village is St. Gile's church, surrounded by thatched cottages, a wonderful bakery, a primary school, an olde village shop and at the far end, the village pub. The population of the village at that time was about three hundred. The Royal Oak Inn was an impressive old building, enrobed in a thick coat of virginia creeper. It thrived on local business. The River Wyle, renowned by trout fishermen, was one hundred yards from the pub.

Providing you were prepared to work hard, running a pub as a tenant with a reputable brewer was regarded as a privilege back then. There was a very long waiting list of applicants (oh, how this changed when the

Pub Companies were formed some twenty years later!). We considered ourselves lucky, and after going through the process of contacting the brewery, were interviewed by a very young area manager. The terms of the tenancy agreement were outlined, most of which went completely over our heads. After assuring him that we could raise the grand sum of four hundred pounds, we were offered a three year tenancy of The Royal Oak Inn, with a rent review at the end of each three year period.

Looking back, it's hard to believe that at this stage we had only seen the pub as customers and had never been behind the scenes. Regardless of this we made an appointment with the existing tenant to look over the pub in detail. After coffee, he gave us a grand tour. The pub was huge, old, dirty, and certainly in need of considerable T.L.C.. However, from the outside, the pub was very eye-catching and attractive. As mentioned, the walls externally were draped in virginia creeper, which was probably as old as the pub. There were white, wooden framed windows, one of which refused to close the whole time we lived there. On the corner of the building there was a sign showing a painted oak tree under the pub name.

The Oak

New Porch

Inside the pub itself, there was a fairly large Public Bar with dark oak wall panels, a long solid wood counter (in need of some repair), and a huge open fireplace. There was also a small Lounge Bar, which had a seperate entrance off a lobby. In the porch was a small hatch for serving 'Off Sales'. This was sometimes called 'The Jug and Bottle' as, in the past, customers would bring a jug or a bottle to be filled with ale.

The cellar was situated under both bars and accessed via a hatch in the floor behind the bar. Immediately behind the public bar was a small private lounge which was, probably, originally a staff rest room. In this room, on one wall, was an oblong glass fronted case with little hinged flaps marked with bedrooms 1, 2, 3, and 4. They didn't work when we lived there, but had obviously been used to summon staff in the past. The kitchen was situated beyond this lounge and was fitted with an electric cooker (with one working ring), a trestle table (once used when hanging wallpaper), and a large chipped sink. A freestanding wood burner was situated in the middle of the kitchen on which pans could be heated. Via a small lobby off the "servants lounge" was a large lounge facing the road. Imagine the stories this grand old building could tell us.

Upstairs, on two levels were seven bedrooms, a bathroom, and a toilet, all very drab! The floors were very uneven and in one bedroom, the bed had a house-brick, placed lengthways under one leg of the bed, to make the bed level! The walls of the rooms were lumpy and also uneven, with holes here and there, "weaping" a chalky powder.

After the brief tour, the existing tenant then proceeded to ply us with stiff drinks to celebrate. He had two drinks to our one, all while serving customers at the same time! This was a salutary lesson for us at an appropriate time. Do *not* drink alcohol while on duty! We later applied this rule to ourselves, and to our staff, throughout our career in the licensed trade.

Having been screened to ensure that we hadn't murdered anyone or robbed any banks (or if we had, had not been caught), we attended a special court in Salisbury. This was to obtain the necessary licence to sell alcohol on and off the premises.

In the ensuing weeks we worked behind the bar on several occasions to obtain some idea of the bar layout and to meet some of the locals. I learned how to change barrels, the difference between a hard and soft spile, and how to whack a brass tap into a barrel with a heavy rubber-headed mallet. We also learned how to clean all the beer lines connected to the cask ales and keg beers. During this introduction period, we met the only current employee, Vicky, who only worked when the former licensees had an evening off. We worked with Vicky one evening and to our amazement she kept her scarf and overcoat on all evening. She explained that it was because the pub was so cold most of the time. We were soon to change this situation.

The Public Bar

We came to the great event of actually moving into our new home and business on March 26th, 1967. In England from 1155 to 1752 the new year began on March 25th. It became the traditional day that contracts between landowners and tenants changed and was aptly called "Lady Day". As a side note, March 25th is also "The Feast of the Annunciation", which commemorates the visit of the archangel Gabriel to the Virgin Mary, during which he informed her that she would be the mother of Jesus Christ. Anyway, the 26th of March continued to be the day that most Pubs changed hands.

Traditionally, a business remained open during the transfer of Tenants. Why this is remains a mystery to me. Remaining open during the transition (one Tenant in, one Tenant out) results in unnecessary stress and confusion. If ever there is a day when a pub should close, it is this one.

While we were moving in, the Dray arrived with our first order of beer, wines and spirits.

"Where do you want this lot, Guv?" Asked a burly drayman.

"Just stick it all in the cellar, I'll sort it later," I replied, already wondering what the dickens I have let us in for. Later, that same afternoon when we were still getting moved in, there was a knock on the front door. I opened the door and was confronted by a very well dressed woman.

"Hello, I'm Lady Parker. I'm your neighbour, and I'm collecting for our dear Doctor who has just retired. Please give generously."

"I only moved into the pub this morning and have never met the Doctor, but here is half a crown," I replied.

Lady Parker took the money and left without saying a word. She and her husband, Lord Parker, were our neighbours for nearly twenty years, but they never once entered the pub. Lady Parker even thought that I was the baker, and blamed me for being late delivering her bread, some fifteen years later!

During our first evening, I was serving behind the bar when I heard one of the locals, Herbie, remark quietly, "Er wunt last long, too skinny, not strong enough!"

He was referring to Kate. How wrong could he be?

GENTLY, GENTLY

Gradually, some order came out of that memorable first day. Our first job was to smarten the old place up. This, of course, was a mammoth task. There were a few very basics that we changed in the first week, one being the removal of spittoons in the Public Bar. Yes, the old codgers chewed tobacco and spat into these aluminium spittoons. In all, this 'smarten up' process took about three years! Kate tackled the kitchen, two lounges, upstairs, the bathroom, one toilet, and seven bedrooms. I decorated both bars from top to bottom during and after opening hours. Trade was so quiet, that it seemed perfectly normal to put a paint brush down, serve someone a pint of beer and then carry on painting. I can remember on several occasions giving a customer a paint brush so that they could give me a hand.

The only heating in the Lounge Bar was from an old two bar electric fire. Any original fireplace had been boarded up behind the electric fire. I investigated, and to our amazement, an imposing Inglenook fireplace had been hidden, complete with seats on either side. We endeavoured to light a fire, hoping that this would be a great feature, but the smoke refused to go up the chimney. We called a builder to investigate. His opinion was that the chimney was so large it required a huge fire to work well. He suggested that a wood burning stove would look good and provide plenty of heat. We took his advice. The wood burner was installed and included a metal chimney of the appropriate size to ensure that the smoke went up rather than down!

Smoking was the norm, and to keep the ceilings in the bars looking 'clean", we painted them nicotine orange. When arranging the bar each day, a large ashtray was positioned every few feet along the counter, and there was an ashtray on each table. In later years, we installed air cleaners to protect us all from second hand smoke, as well as to clean the air. The filters in the air cleaners were changed every three months, and in that time they oozed nicotine slime.

The cellar was cold and damp, with a sweet musty smell. It was ideal for keeping real ales, but the walls were thick with mould. It housed the most enormous slugs and a few tiny lizards. The strange thing was, the slugs were attracted to the red labels on the Watney Mann, brown ale, bottles and only those. Naturally, we told folk that we had 'Mann eating slugs' in the cellar! We gradually treated the whole cellar with special paint and it became sparkling clean, but it was still an ideal temperature for real ale, at 11-13 degrees Celsius.

Our vision was to run a pub where everyone was welcome and felt at ease. What we inherited was a largely male clientele, including a fairly large number of young lads. Some of the latter were a bit rough, and their language was crude, to say the least. This didn't fit our vision, and I didn't want Kate, or any other lady in the pub, listening to such bad language. I decided that I would wear a dickybow tie when working on the bar, to gently encourage a bit more formality. I felt a real prat to begin with, but it had the desired effect.

"Not going in that snobby joint!" John, one of our older regulars, had heard in the village.

We were not disappointed. We had obtained a good result without any confrontation. Having been in the Royal Navy and mixing with sailors,' I was certainly not a prude. I could probably use language that would shock most people, but there is a time and place, and we didn't want our lovely pub to be the place.

FOOD IN PUBS?

The only food available in the pub when we moved in was bread, cheese, and pickles. A pickled egg in a bag of crisps was a luxury! The menu, in its entirety, consisted of a Ploughman's Lunch. This was fresh crusty bread (from the village bakery), a slab of cheddar cheese, butter, and pickles. The village had a superb bakery, where they baked large cottage loaves six days a week. We sold about twenty Ploughman's Lunches a week, but only at lunchtimes.

Our intention was to gradually introduce more food, as trade increased. Bearing in mind that our total takings on our first Saturday was one pound, one shilling, and two pence, this was going to be slow progress. However, our very first attempt at selling "hot" food was an immediate success. Sausages, pre-cooked and kept warm on a metal tray by 'night light' candles, were served in slices on cocktail sticks. These went down very well! The local lads, who had decided to remain regular customers, particularly enjoyed this first batch, as it was free!

We had heard from Kate's mum in London that a local pub near her had started selling chicken and chips, served in little wicker baskets. We managed to source some wicker baskets, and we purchased a deep fat fryer. Kate prepared the baskets, lined with greaseproof paper, with fresh fries served alongside a sizzling, golden brown piece of tender fried chicken. Basket meals were an immediate success and in no time our range of hot food in baskets included breaded fish, scampi, sausages, king prawns, and the ever popular chicken. Word spread fast, and more customers came in to try this new phenomena at "The Oak". "The Oak" was becoming the name the locals used for the pub and we went along with it.

The downside to hot food was that several locals announced that they did not approve of food smells in a Public bar.

"It's not a bloody cafe!" Announced one such local before he promptly walked out.

We were at The Royal Oak Inn for over twenty years and although those folk who disapproved of food in pubs, lived in the village, they never came back in. Obstinate buggers! The funny thing was that there were three pubs within walking distance to the village, and so these people just moved to the others. However, as food in pubs became more and more popular, most pubs in the area started experimenting with a small menu.

Our basket meals really took off. On one occasion we ran out of fresh chicken. Kate and I pondered our predicament, as we had a full bar of hungry customers. Using my initiative, I proceeded to take six frozen chickens into the garden shed and cut them into quarters with my hand saw. We continued to plonk them into the deep fat fryer, giving them a bit longer to cook all the way through. Fortunately, only one customer asked for his chicken to be cooked a bit more as it was still a bit frozen in the middle! We had not been on any courses in health and hygiene at this point. These courses are really necessary to run a catering operation, and we later obtained the appropriate qualifications along with key kitchen staff.

On Saturday evenings, we were so crowded that people often had to stand outside to eat their meal, as there were no tables left inside the Public Bar.

Basket Meal

Kate was already a good cook, but we realised that the way forward was definitely to serve more and more food. Kate took a ''Cordon Bleu' cookery course that was available on a weekly home basis (no online in those days). For two years, she studied and practiced her cooking skills. Gradually, our menu increased in volume and quality, as did the customer base. We also obtained accolades in several food guides.

Chef at Work

OUR FIRST CLEANER

It wasn't long before we required someone to help with cleaning the bars. We advertised in the local shop window and within minutes we had an applicant. A young lady from the village. She started the next morning. We gave her instructions and cleaning equipment, and she duly started her chores. When I came into the bar later, she was on her hands and knees facing away from me. Her very short skirt had ridden up her back, and I was confronted with a dirty pair of knickers, that were full of holes with areas of pink bum poking through! Not a pretty sight. I backed away quietly.

Later, I was behind the bar getting ready to open and she was still cleaning by a window when a group of lads from the village tried to open the pub door. She looked through the window and to my horror yelled,

"F--k off, we are not open yet!"

Thank goodness they were locals who knew her. The final straw came when she finished cleaning and asked if she could have a loan of twenty pounds. I didn't give her any money, and apart from a short skirt she also had a very short career at The Oak! Although she never worked at the pub again, she applied for every job that we ever advertised for. Throughout our career at The Oak, we had many cleaners, but none that compared to her! Bless her.

YOU CAN'T PLEASE EVERYONE

The Oak's dart team was a major weekly event in the early days. It was taken so seriously that the 'stars' expected to be collected from their homes, delivered to either the home or away game venue, then duly returned to their home at the end of the evening. Also, at away games, I was expected to attend the match and treat my team to drinks all round. One evening, not a match evening, two of the team were practicing in the Public Bar. They had moved three tables out of the way in order to have a clear sight of the dartboard. Our food trade was just taking off and those three tables represented twelve people, most of them eating. The two lads playing darts would at most buy three pints each, all evening. Although I liked the lads, we were not running this business for fun, so the darts team had to go. Naturally, this caused considerable angst, and we lost a few regulars as a result. I'll bet that they called me some interesting names, but at the end of the day, we did need to make some profit.

My dad, a retired Policeman, had advised us from the start that if we tried to please everyone, we would end up pleasing no one. For about two years we did not employ anyone. However, we were gradually becoming busier, particularly on weekends, and one Saturday evening I was serving at the bar and Kate was in the kitchen. I was struggling to pull pints fast enough. Suddenly one of our regular customers appeared by my side and started serving customers.

"Thanks, John," I muttered.

"I reckoned that If I was ever going to get a drink I had better help myself!" John replied.

He was our first employee (starting right then and there), and he became a very close friend. He was with us for more than ten years.

John was a good looking (according to Kate), burly blond lad who had lived in the village all of his life.

One evening, after we had closed, John walked all round the village with me and named every resident. When we returned to the pub, we realised that we had left the main pub door wide open with all of the lights on, with the cash register unattended. Happy days!

Every evening, punctually at six pm, it was opening time. I would open the pub door and an old chap would wander in, order a bottle of Guiness, and then proceed to play the gaming machine with a vengeance. John was on bar duty with me one evening, when the old guy came in. John served him his Guiness and the old chap proceeded to play the fruit machine as usual.

"He's a strange old cock, isn't he?" I whispered to John.

"Yes, he is," he replied, "he's my Dad!"

No sign of recognition or conversation had ever passed between them. Fifty years ago there was definitely a more formal relationship between a father and his children, so this was not unusual.

We were talking later that evening and agreed that although politics and religion were often heatedly discussed by customers, it was important that we diplomatically did not become involved. John advised that another observation best avoided was the resemblance of people from different families.

"Now you mention it, a lot of folk from different families have very similar features." I mentioned wryly.

John explained later that evening, that in a little village, like Great Wishford, most people lived and worked in and around the village which resulted in a certain amount of hanky panky taking place. He continued to inform me that it was common on Sunday afternoons for many folk to take a stroll in Grovely wood, and that is where this often occurred. Rumour has it that in certain areas there was a layer of rubber beneath the leaves, he added with a huge grin.

Grovely wood is one of the largest woodlands in southern England and is situated along a chalk ridge one mile behind "The Royal Oak". It is a beautiful wood of sweet chestnut, hazel, specimen conifers, fine old beech trees, and huge old oak trees. There are also many romantic glades!

Oak Apples or Oak Galls are found in the oak trees in Grovely wood. Interestingly, they are not fruit but round objects caused by kinds of wasps. Although Oak Apple Day is normally associated with Charles II's escape from the roundheads by hiding in an oak tree, Oak Apple Day in Great Wishford had more to do with village rights.

REAL CHARACTERS

Several of the regular customers were real characters. One named Len had been a sniper in World War I, and in his eighties was becoming a bit forgetful. Often he would look up and say,

"Tell me when I've had my three pints, as I lose count."

He normally came in about mid-morning, and one day when he hadn't arrived, I started to worry. In the end, I asked one of his neighbours if he had seen him.

"Yes," he replied, "he was on his way home when I passed him. I assumed that he had already been to the pub."

Len duly arrived on schedule the next morning and so I quizzed him about his absence the day before. After giving it some considerable thought, he realised that on his way to the pub he had tried to light a cigarette. It was windy, and the match that he was trying to light it with kept blowing out. He turned round to face the way he had come and with the wind behind him, lit his cigarette then continued to walk back home! Until I mentioned it, he had completely forgotten that he had not reached the pub the day before.

Len often rode his old bike to the pub. Some days, when we closed for the night, we would find his bike leaning against the wall outside. We would bring it inside and put it back out for him the next morning. Len would walk in the next day and ask how his bike had got there! Sometimes he just forgot that he had ridden his bike, or maybe he was too wobbly after three pints, and decided to walk back home.

After the war, Len had resumed his career as a stone mason and was involved in building Stoford Bridge, the main road bridge into the village. He also was a bit of a gentleman's hairdresser in his spare time.

One story he liked to tell was about old Jake. Apparently Jake had a really bad nervous twitch and just could not keep his head still. When Len tried to cut his hair, he said to Jake,

"I'll keep the scissors still, Jake, while you moves yer 'ed."

OAK APPLE DAY

Our first major event after taking over The Royal Oak Inn was Oak Apple Day. May 29th marks this day for Great Wishford. John filled us in on how it affected the pub and I swotted up a bit to find out more.

Oak Apple Day in Great Wishford had nothing to do with King Charles II escaping from capture by hiding in an oak tree. Here, it was a common right to collect wood from Grovely wood, situated behind the pub. The tradition is said to date back to 1603, when the charter of rights to collect wood in the Royal Forest of Grovely, was confirmed in the Forest Court. Villagers travel to the wood on Oak Apple Day to collect a live bough to display outside of their house. Four ladies from the village travel to Salisbury Cathedral, where they dance on the green singing "Grovely, Grovely, and all Grovely". While we were at "The Oak" not many people actually collected wood throughout the year, but Oak Apple day was still a big occasion in the village.

Oak Apple Day

A large field, situated in the middle of the village, was regarded as the Oak Apple field and was the focus of most of the day's events, with a lunch, fete, small fair, Morris dancers, and a bar provided by The Royal Oak. A couple of local lads were employed and we set up a crude bar in a large tent in the Oak Apple field. During that first Oak Apple Day (for us), one of the main attractions was a military band from one of the local army barracks. They duly arrived by coach, dressed in their smart uniforms and proceeded to play a few tunes, very professionally, before lunch. They were certainly a great attraction as they marched smartly up and down the field. However, during the lunch break, they imbibed heavily at our bar and quite a few were very much the worse for wear! They had to play again during the afternoon.

"Quick march!" Shouted the Band Master, and off they went, playing a bit off key. Halfway up the field, the Band Master commanded, "About turn!"

Most of the band turned smartly, but unfortunately, quite a few did not, so were confronted with their colleagues coming straight towards them. The ensuing collisions resulted in total shambles. Some members of the band even fell over and dropped their instruments and hats.

The crowd howled with laughter and cheered enthusiastically, much to the amusement of the band players, but certainly *not* the Band Master. He tried unsuccessfully to restore order, but the soldiers were just too far gone. That was the end of their involvement and the coach, taking them back to Barracks, left shortly after.

The pub was much busier than normal but we muddled through. We became more involved and more professional in future years, and, needless to say, from then on, any attending military band on Oak Apple Day was forbidden to visit our beer tent! That was a shame really, as they had certainly been the star attraction that year!

Another major attraction was the Morris Dancers who performed in front of the pub during the festivities. This English Folk Dance was accompanied by one member playing an accordian. The Morris men were dressed in white, wore bells on their shins, and danced, waving white handkerchiefs and sticks that they bashed together. This tradition can be traced as far back as 1448 where it is recorded that the Goldsmith Company paid seven shillings to Morris Dancers in London. However, this dance became less popular until about 1899. Then in the 1950s and especially the 1960s there was an explosion of new dance teams. Some teams were women and some mixed, although all the teams that we saw outside The Oak were men. They were certainly a great attraction to the village, and importantly to us, great beer drinkers.

Yet another annual event that drew a huge crowd was the Greasy Pole contest and tug o' war contest between the Swann Inn and The Royal Oak. A huge tree trunk spanned the River Wyle and brave contestants, including me and the landlord of the Swan, bashed seven bells out of each other with a wet sack, stuffed with straw, in an endeavor to dislodge the other into the river. The contestants sat on the log that had been soaked in water to make it very slippery, hence the term Greasy Pole.

Morris Dancers

Greasy Pole Competition

Oak Apple Parade

THE GUESTS ARRIVE

Our next major event was the arrival of three fishermen who came each year, and stayed on a full board basis at the pub, during the fly fishing season, to fish for trout on the River Wyle. They were all members of the Wilton Fly Fishing Club. It was, and still is, an exclusive club with membership limited to just forty-five members per year. Most members remain for many years, so there is normally a considerable waiting list. No day tickets for non members are available. Members are dedicated fly fishermen, keen to fish the challenging waters of the River Wyle, for wild trout and grayling, using dry fly or nymph, upstream only. No stocked fish here! The club had a seven mile stretch of the river and it was policed and maintained by a full time riverkeeper. Norman Smith was the keeper while we were at The Oak. He was a charming, knowledgeable, and fastidious keeper well respected by the members.

The first guest to arrive was Mr. Chris Wrey. He had phoned a few days earlier to confirm his stay ,and to ask if we could make room for his 'Rolls' in our garage. He was an ex-director of a large tobacco company. He duly arrived in a very ancient, grey Austin Mini!

The next day Dr. Doyne Bell and Mr. Nick Roughead arrived. If you can envisage the three men as depicted in the illustrations from the PickWick Papers, this would be the perfect description of Mr.

Roughead, Dr. Bell, and Mr. Wrey. They were utterly charming and extremely plump! Dr. Bell had been a very well regarded paediatric consultant in London. When he realised that Kate had been a nurse, he called her "Nurse Kate" from then on. Nick Roughead's claim to fame was that he had been a Rating in the Royal Navy and had refused to take rank. In 1937, he had also been the Captain of Scotland's Rugby team. He fished for trout all around the world, and left a complete fishing kit in each of his favourite venues. (He actually left me his 'Oak' fly fishing rods and flies, when he died. Hand-crafted rods made in Scotland that I still use to this day). I'm not sure how they managed it, but when I told the 'fishermen' that I enjoyed fly fishing, they made me an honorary member of the club and I fished regularly.

Nick Roughead had been staying annually at The Oak since 1938 and had kept a diary of every fish that he had caught in the river Wyle, up until the year before he died in 1975. I still have this diary, and there is a page in it titled 'War Intervened' and it mentions that he joined the Royal Navy from May 20th, 1941 until September 28th, 1945, as an Able Seaman. He served on HMS Indomitable, HMS Nelson, and HMS Kingsmill. He never spoke of this chapter in his life, except that he had refused to take any promotion from Able Seaman. I only found these details from this fishing diary, and apart from his time in The Royal Navy, he had regarded fishing for trout as his 'work'. When this book has been published, the diary will be given to the Wilton Fly Fishing Club.

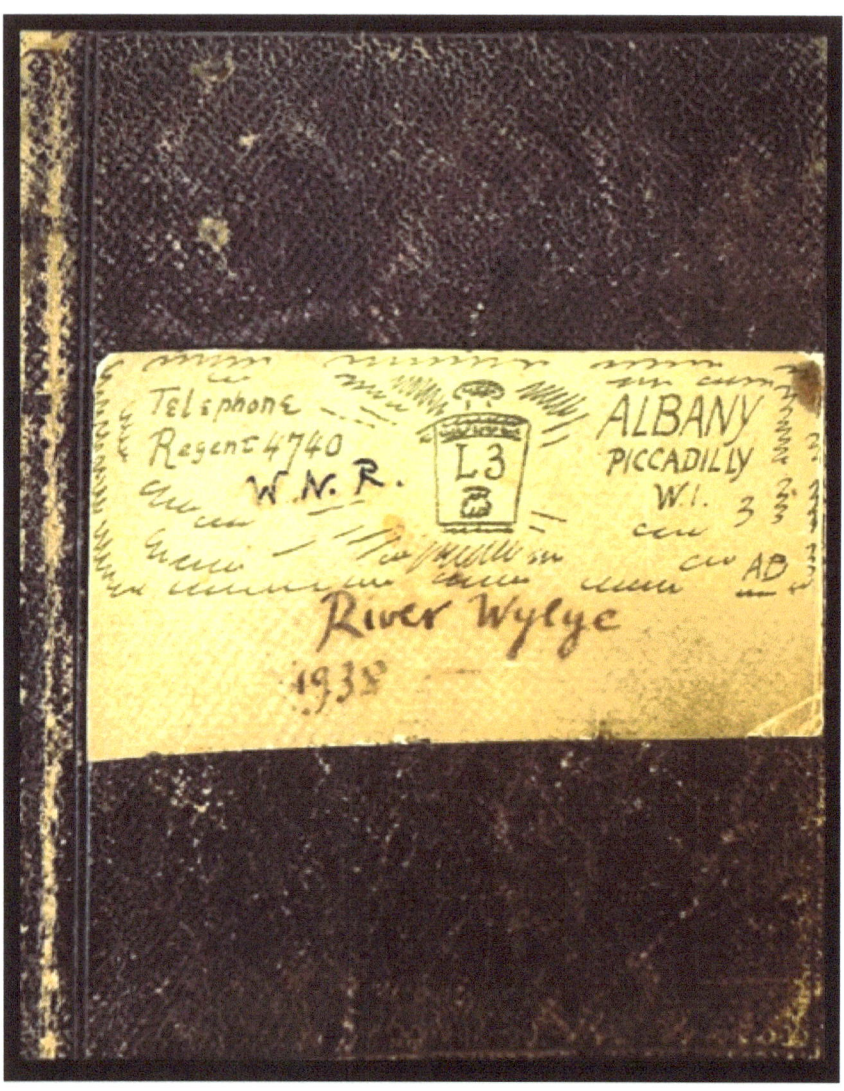

The Diary

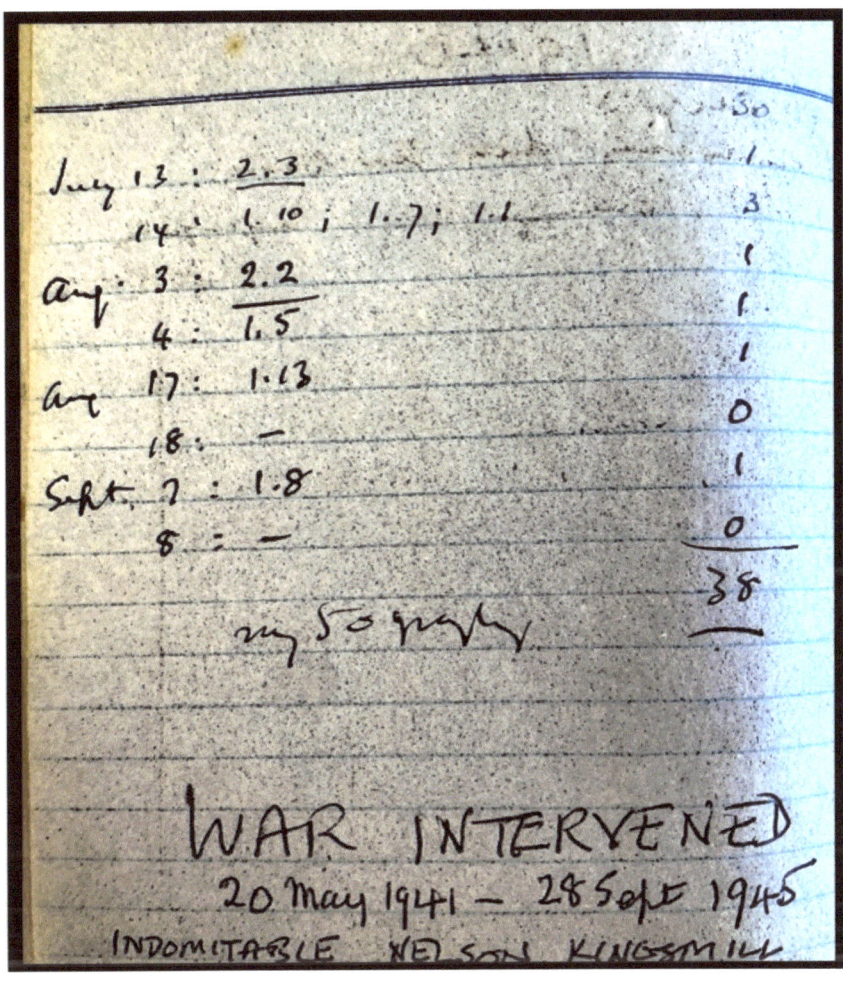

'War Intervened' Entry

Mr. Roughead goes to work

Nick Roughead is buried in St. Giles graveyard, which is situated behind the pub. We also discovered that his father, also W. N. Roughead, had been a solicitor, and then a famous author specialising in notorious murder cases. He wrote numerous books, and was a great friend of Hilaire Belloc, the author and poet.

No Room at the Inn

Mr. Wrey, straight from a wedding to fishing

The fishermen stayed on and off throughout the fly fishing season, which is April to October for trout. Grayling were also prevalent in the river and could be fished for all year. During the early days, Nick Roughhead regularly came for a while during the winter to fish for grayling and pike. As they didn't know in advance exactly when they would be staying, but wanted their rooms to always be available, they booked, and paid for them for the whole fly fishing season, well in advance. This was a real financial bonus for us as we were just starting a new business with some ambitious ideas for introducing more extensive catering, which involved some expensive catering equipment.

The fisherman had interesting drink preferences. Mr. Wrey only drank 'gentleman's measures' of Haig whisky. Nick Roughead liked a large gin and dry vermouth with lemon zest, and Dr. Bell preferred whisky and water. Dr. Bell was writing a book during his stays, and only wrote by candlelight, which he regarded as soothing. He believed that he was suffering from angina, and therefore only drank whisky to expand his blood vessels!

Quite often, when they had been fishing they would settle in the small lounge bar, smoking and drinking. I had a little book behind the bar and they would help themselves to drinks and record whatever they had in this book. This worked reasonably well, but a couple of events spring to mind.

Sometimes, during the process of cleaning the beer lines, I would leave them to soak, with the cleaning solution in the pipes, well into the afternoon, prior to rinsing with clean water later. On one occasion the three gentlemen had decided to try a pint of beer for a change. Later, when I came to rinse the pipes with fresh water in preparation for the evening, Dr. Bell announced very seriously,

"We think that there is something wrong with the beer today, we couldn't drink it."

Yes, they had tried to drink the cleaning fluid!

On another occasion they had also decided to have a beer in the afternoon. When I came to serve in the bar later, the floor was awash with beer and when I went down to the cellar, there was several inches of beer sloshing about on the cellar floor. They had pulled three pints of beer from a keg of Watneys Red Barrel, then left the tap on and consequently poured nearly twenty two gallons of beer onto the bar floor.

"Oh dear," said Mr. Wrey. "Charge us the full price for the whole keg, that might teach us to be more careful."

EELS!

The Fishermen brought the trout and grayling that they had caught back each evening, and either gave them to the locals or asked Kate to cook them for their evening meal, or breakfast. I gather club rules for trout now are 'catch and release'. One day a local had given Nick Roughead two decent sized eels. There was an eel house situated on the river about half a mile upstream from Stoford bridge. This was no longer in use, but these eel houses date back to the 1800s and were built to trap the eels as they migrate to breed. Eels were still quite plentiful in the river and provided a regular meal for some folk.

Eel House

Nick Roughead didn't fancy the eels for dinner and he informed us that he would keep them somewhere safe until morning. We assumed that he would put them in a bucket of water. The next morning, when Kate asked him if he would like the eels cooked for breakfast, he replied somewhat sheepishly that they were dead. Having only one upstairs toilet, which was some distance from their bedrooms, each of the fishermen had a potty under their bed. These potty's were locally known as "Gazunders" as they "gaz under yer" bed. These were used to save trips to the toilet during the night. Nick had put the eels in his potty with some water and then forgotten them. He had then peed on them several times during the night. Luckily they didn't bite him!

Poor Eels!

DON'T LOOK UP

The locals were well acquainted with "the fishermen," as they were fondly known. Mr. Wrey's bedroom was in the front of the pub and the local lads had learned not to loiter under his bedroom window as he was known to go to bed early, have a pee in his potty, then calmly empty it out of the window.

One Oak Apple Day evening, this ritual came in very handy. About twenty lads from Wilton had been drinking heavily most of the afternoon and evening and although I had managed to get them out at closing time, they continued to be very rowdy outside the pub entrance. Suddenly, the contents of an ashtray landed on them, closely followed by you know what!

CAR ON FIRE

One morning, before opening time, a young man came rushing in the front door yelling,

"Do you have a fire extinguisher? My car is on fire!"

I grabbed a small extinguisher from behind the bar and went to investigate. Sure enough, his Volkswagen was on fire, in the middle of the road just outside the pub. Fortunately, no one was inside the car. My extinguisher had little effect and so I called 999 for Fire and Police. We had a larger fire extinguisher close to the kitchen and so I grabbed that next. Before I had finished using it, the car just exploded into a huge ball of flames. The fire brigade arrived quite quickly and as the car was not salvageable they just concentrated on extinguishing the flames.

While this was happening the local policeman arrived. He came over to me with a huge grin on his face.

"What's so funny?" I asked him.

"It couldn't have happened to a nicer chap," he replied sarcastically. "He has been a real nuisance to us for some time, as he has been driving that damned car recklessly through the villages," he chuckled. "Good riddance!"

I wasn't amused. The guy had not been insured and I had used two fire extinguishers for a fire not related to the pub so consequently was unable to claim on my insurance, under those circumstances. It did, however, create quite a bit of interest in the village that morning, so trade was brisk.

ANOTHER FIRE

Not long after the basket meals had become popular, Kate had been busy in the kitchen when my brother and his wife came to visit. Kate and Jo, my sister in law, were both pregnant at the time and adjourned upstairs to compare bumps. Unfortunately, Kate had left a deep fat fryer on the maximum temperature setting and it overflowed and caught fire. Dave, my brother, and I were playing snooker in what was then the old Club Room, when we spotted smoke billowing from the kitchen.

We rushed to the kitchen door, and as soon as we opened it, a ball of flames whooshed out. We both ran to the front of the pub yelling frantically for everyone to get out. I dashed upstairs to warn the girls to get Nick, our young son, and Mr. Wrey, outside urgently. Dave had called the fire brigade and grabbed the fire extinguisher from behind the bar (a new one!), and we both proceeded back to the yard. We aimed the extinguisher through the kitchen door but it was too hot, and the flames leaping from the kitchen door forced us to retreat hastily.

Fortunately, the fire brigade arrived quite quickly and several firemen dashed straight into the kitchen. They immediately came back out coughing and spluttering. Once the proper gear had been donned, they went back in and soon had the fire under control. Having checked that it was completely extinguished, they disconnected the electrical supply and left. Kate, Jo, and little Nick were still huddled in the car park with a few customers.

"Is everyone OK?" I asked, "And what about you Mr. Wrey?"

He replied that he was fine because during the war he had been taught an important rule. This was, in an emergency, ensure that you have,

"Testicles, spectacles, wallet, and watch."

He reckoned with these in place, he could survive most things!

Dave, my brother, was a qualified electrician and having established that the electricity to the remains of the kitchen was safely disconnected, managed to reconnect the power to the rest of the pub. We went back into the bar, which was still full of wispy smoke, and there, to our horror, was old Herbie, still sitting at the bar clutching his pint of beer.

"Why on earth are you still in here, Herbie?" I said somberly.

"Guarding the till." He replied very seriously.

Herbie After the Fire

The kitchen was a total write off, but fortunately the fire crew had prevented any damage beyond the confines of the kitchen. The big extractor fan situated behind the fryers was a molten blob in the car park. Although the destruction was a very scary experience, it provided the opportunity to upgrade the kitchen, literally from top to bottom. We were just beginning to expand the catering operation, so now we installed stainless steel work-tops, three new fryers, two microwave ovens and a Mealstream, which was a powerful microwave oven combined with a convection oven. The two existing commercial ovens were damaged, but fortunately could be refurbished. New commercial flooring was also installed.

Our insurance policy enabled Mundy's, the village builders, to repair the ceiling, and redecorate. Consequently, not a huge amount of business was lost. In fact, the fire had created a lot of interest, so beer sales were brisk. We were back operating the catering side of the business within five weeks.

Mr. Wrey was the only resident at the time. The evening following the fire he was in the public bar chatting to the locals and they were swapping tales and telling jokes. His favorite story went like this. He had an old friend named Seth who was a wealthy farmer living in Devon. He had recently married a beautiful young girl from the village. Not long after the marriage, Seth was in the local pub when several of his mates asked him how he liked married life.

"It's terrible," he answered. "I can't keep me 'ands off 'er."

"That's perfectly normal, Seth, she is gorgeous," they replied.

"Well, I really don't like it, it's disgusting," he replied.

The next day, in the pub again, one of the locals asked Seth how things were going.

"Dreadful. Me 'ands are all over 'er," he grumbled.

This went on for some time, then one evening, Seth came into the bar with a big smile on his face.

"You look happy Seth," one of his pals observed.

"Yes, I am," he replied with a smile, "I've solved the problem with me 'ands."

"How did you do that?" His friend asked, to everyone's amusement.

"Easily," he replied, "I sacked me 'ands and bought a tractor!"

CHRISTMAS AND BOXING DAY

Christmas lunchtime was fairly busy, and the tradition was that each customer who came in was given their first drink free of charge. This was called 'on the house'. The idea was that this gesture was a way of expressing our appreciation to the locals who had supported us during the year. We were still new to the business and did not really recognise everyone, but soon became aware that a few strangers were asking for their free drink. Several even tried to get a second free drink by ordering one from me and the second from Kate. One of our regulars advised that although they were strangers to us, they were known by him, and that they visited as many pubs on Christmas Day as they could, to take advantage of the free drinks. A typical example of a few spoiling something for many. From then on we thanked our locals individually with a free drink.

No food was available the first Christmas Day that we were at the pub. I remember that a small young local lad, no more than eight years old, appeared at the off-sales hatch and asked if he could buy something to eat. This was Christmas Day at lunchtime! Typing this still brings tears to my eyes. The poor little chap had been given two shillings to go off and find something to eat on Christmas Day, while his parents went from pub to pub getting as many free drinks as they could. Needless to say, Kate nipped into the kitchen, prepared fish and chips and gave them to the little chap, then sat him in the lounge bar with a large coke. This was probably the best meal that he had had for ages, plus he had two shillings in his pocket!

We didn't open on Christmas Day again.

Boxing Day involved another tradition that we continued and expanded on in future years. A carol service was held during the lunchtime session and Kate and I provided free mince pies while the village vicar led the carols. This was an extremely popular and festive occasion, but had an interesting outcome. Bearing in mind that at that time we only had the Public Bar and the small Lounge Bar with a total capacity of about sixty people, this was the first time that we had been full. The result was that the weight of all these bodies caused the old oak beams supporting the Public Bar floor to bow so much that the door to the off-sales porch jammed firmly until some people left via the toilets.

I contacted the brewery's surveyor soon afterwards and he duly came to inspect.

"Nothing to worry about," he advised, and departed.

Further involvement with brewery surveyors led me to believe that their brief was to spend as little time as possible on any of the Pubs that their company owned.

I was still concerned, so I asked a company that specialised in pest control for an independent survey of the premises. Their report indicated severe dry rot, wet rot, deathwatch beetle, weevil, woodworm, cockroaches, and mice in the pub, and rats under the old Club Room, which was situated across the back yard. There were a lot of us living at The Oak at that time!

The mice problem was confirmed by the fact that we had placed a Christmas tree upstairs for young Nick, and adorned it with little chocolate, foil covered, decorations. The next morning every single one had been chewed by mice! This report resulted in the oak beams in the cellar (that had bowed during the carol service on Boxing Day), being replaced by steel joists. The huge wooden oak beams that had originally been installed in an old ship, had been irreparably weakened by death watch beetles.

During this eradication process, the pub was closed for three days as chemicals, which created noxious fumes, were injected into the walls and behind the wood panel, to eliminate the cockroaches. All the remaining wooden oak beams were treated to kill the deathwatch beetles. Prior to this treatment, it was actually possible to hear the beatles. When the males were trying to attract a female, they made a ticking sound. I didn't realise at the time that this sound had been regarded as an omen of impending death to people hearing it. Fortunately, this didn't apply to us, but the treatment did to them!

The old guy that came to deal with the rats squirted some nasty gas under the floorboards of the Club room to kill them. Unfortunately, he hadn't realized that his little dog had rushed to the other side of the building as he did this. Yes, he killed the rats and his dog.

RESTAURANT NUMBER ONE

The large Lounge, situated on the ground floor, was rarely used. We decided to adapt it into a trial restaurant. We installed four tables, each seating four diners, and a small menu was displayed in both bars. This was an immediate success. After a couple of years, as our reputation for food increased and we became more professional in our approach to the business, we became aware that this room was not adequate. The Club Room (in the back yard), was a decent size, but not used to its potential, so we decided to make it our new restaurant.

The Club Room, up until then, had only been used once a week as a "Buff Lodge". Let me explain.

The Royal Antediluvian Order of Buffaloes (RAOB) started in a Tavern in 1822. It's motto is "no man is at all times wise". The name Buffaloes came from a song at the time, "We'll Chase the Buffaloes". Members promise to assist mem
bers of the local community in times of difficulty or need. Regions throughout the country and in many countries had units called Lodges. The one using the Club room was quite small and consisted of about a dozen members from the village. Although they regarded the Club room as theirs, it wasn't, and we needed to expand our business. So, unfortunately the Buffaloes had to graze elsewhere. The members of the Lodge, although disappointed, were very understanding and co-operated fully.

We redecorated the Club room and installed a window at the far end, adjacent to the carpark. I built four tables to accommodate four diners and four tables for two. The room was damp and cold, so we installed a woodburner with a back boiler that heated two radiators. Our landlords decided to help us (for additional rent). Builders were engaged to convert old garages that adjoined the Club Room into an integral part of the catering operation. We added an additional kitchen and a large storage area. A small bar was created and I fitted it out with mirrors, wine racks, and optic shelves together with provision for a glass washer and ice making machine. I also built work tables and work tops as Kate, the chef, requested.

Advertisements in the local paper, along with word of mouth, quickly started to bring business to the restaurant. Staffing became an issue, as now we were running two kitchens in the evenings. The pub kitchen was where bar snacks were prepared while a comprehensive menu was prepared in the restaurant kitchen. Consequently, we needed additional bar staff as well as kitchen staff for both sectors. Our theory, which generally worked, was that we would create a reputation for paying higher wages than other establishments in the area. As a result, we hoped to recruit reliable people. Weekend staff were paid more, as these were the peak sessions and the staff worked harder. However, we insisted that all staff rotated so that everyone occasionally worked a weekend. Another rule that we introduced was that once we had a compliment of about fifteen, staff arranged their own replacement if they needed to change their session. Then we decided to smarten the appearance of the staff. The men were required to wear white shirts, and dark trousers.The ladies wore white tops and black skirts, provided by us. This uniform was for bar staff and we provided white aprons for kitchen staff.

Saturday evenings were our busiest session. Often there were up to twenty staff involved and it was past midnight before we had finished and cleaned up. Occasionally, we would all wind down with a drink. On several occasions we enjoyed a chinese takeaway which one member had picked up. This created a great team spirit. We employed a large number of staff during our time at "The Oak," and most remained good friends for many years as we went our different ways.

UKLF

United Kingdom Land Forces or UKLF, was a large military establishment, based in Wilton, some six miles from The Oak. The base was situated on land once belonging to the Wilton Estate. During the second world war, Wilton House was requisitioned as the new HQ of Southern Command. The Pembroke Arms hotel became the officers' mess and the canteen was run by Lady Pembroke with a team of helpers. Much of the planning for D-day was done from Wilton House.

UKLF became the source of a variety of interesting experiences. They regularly booked the small Lounge Bar for a private lunchtime refreshment break when they were having high level meetings at their Wilton offices. These sessions were booked well in advance and often were preceded with Soldiers checking the Lounge Bar with sniffer dogs. At this time, during the early seventies, precautions were still in place due to the Irish Republican Army still being active. UKLF were also responsible for many social events involving troops returning from various activities around the world.

One was for about forty extremely athletic looking soldiers. The restaurant was booked to provide a three course meal, but no alcohol. We thought that this was a bit unusual. However, they were a truly amazing group and extremely well behaved. After the main course they proceeded to spend the rest of the evening speaking Russian! We never knew what regiment they were from. Rumour had it that they were Special Air Service, but whoever they were, we were honored to serve them.

Another group, well remembered, were from a regiment of Coldstream Guards. An extremely well spoken young officer came to make arrangements for some of his soldiers to come for drinks and snacks one summer's evening. Apparently, they had recently finished a tour in Ireland. I was a bit dubious, as a few weeks earlier we had a group of about twenty young soldiers in the restaurant and I had to ask them to leave as they were becoming rowdy and aggressive. I mentioned this to the young officer and he assured me that 'his' soldiers would be fine.

"I will be with them, so don't worry, sir," he added.

On the designated evening a big army lorry drew up outside and forty young lads disembarked noisily. They were a great bunch, and if any one of them became too boisterous, one look from the young Officer was all that was needed. The pub toilets were accessed via the Public Bar, so these young soldiers had to go through the Public bar on quite a few occasions. This caused great excitement with the young ladies that were in the bar as the soldiers proceeded to chat them up in a gentle and inoffensive manner. Although they were drinking heavily, they did seem to have very weak bladders from the number of visits to the toilet. We assumed that the word had spread that the soldiers were coming, as more young ladies were in the bar that evening than usual!

When the time came for them to leave, the Officer said, "Right men, that's it, outside, now. In the truck."

Without hesitation, they downed their drinks and quietly left. It was a beautiful summer's evening and, as all of the windows were wide open, most of them went out via the window. However, they blotted their impeccable behaviour by stopping their lorry on stoford bridge then lining up to pee over the wall, into the river!

Although basket meals were our introduction to pub catering, more imaginative dishes progressively became popular, not only in the restaurant, but in the bars as well. One lunchtime there were a few customers from UKLF enjoying sandwiches in the small lounge bar, when one said.

"Something smells good, what is it?"

I said, "It's faggots that Kate is cooking for the family."

"I love faggots," he replied, "if I bring some friends by later in the week, could we have some?"

We agreed, and the men thoroughly enjoyed them on their return visit. From this chance beginning, faggots became a top seller for many years. We made more than three hundred portions weekly using a traditional recipe, including caul fat to wrap them in.

THE GUN

One evening, Kate and I were working in the restaurant and a young man called Richard was working on the bar in the pub. We only had about eight customers in the restaurant and Richard had advised us via the internal telephone that there were about ten local lads in the bar. Later that evening, the internal phone in the restaurant rang. I was about to serve a bottle of wine, but decided to answer the phone first.

"Quick!" Yelled a very anxious Richard," Come quick, there is a guy in the bar with a gun!"

"You are joking?" I replied laughing.

"I'm f-----g not !" He gasped. "Get here quick!" He said, slamming the phone down.

I decided to go see what was going on via the toilet block that connected the bar to the restaurant. Gently opening the toilet door I could see that one of the local lads had spotted me. I waved him over.

"That bloke at the bar is crazy, he has a gun and he threatened us with it!" He explained.

I said nothing, backed out, went into the pub kitchen and dialled 999. When I explained, in a very shaky voice, I was quickly put through to the police and told that they were on the way. By then Richard had joined me in the pub kitchen and refused emphatically to go back to the bar! I peered into the bar once more and the guy was pacing up and down, with his beer untouched on the counter. There was no sign of a gun though. Fortunately, no one else had come into the pub at this stage and the group of local lads were still huddled quietly at the far end of the bar.

In a very short time (although it seemed ages), a police car swept into the car park. Two policemen came into the kitchen via the backyard entrance and Richard and I explained the situation.

"Right," said one of the Policemen, "you go into the bar, go up to the guy and ask him to leave."

"You can't be serious!" I replied. "What if the bugger shoots me?"

"We will be right behind you, so don't worry," he said grimly.

I approached the man very reluctantly, but before I had said a word, both Policemen grabbed him, and a gun did appear. They manhandled him out of the bar and into the toilet and very professionally splayed him against the wall, legs apart, and hands above his head. He struggled without a sound and one of the Policemen handed me the gun and said,

"Get this out of the way quick!"

I was supposed to be helping Kate in the restaurant. I was also waiting on eight diners. Of course, they were all oblivious of what was going on in the Public Bar. I rushed back into the restaurant, still shaking and feeling guilty at abandoning Kate and my customers. There was a small bar area in the restaurant, and without thinking, I deposited the gun on the counter, grabbed the bottle of wine that I had been about to serve when the phone rang, and went to the patient customer.

"I'm sorry about the delay," I mumbled and proceeded to pour the wine. My hands were shaking so badly that one customer asked if I was nervous.

"Sir," I said "when you have finished your meal, I will try and explain what has just happened and you won't believe it!"

When I returned to the bar, Richard and the local lads were now recounting how very brave they had all been. Apparently, the Policemen had cuffed the man, retrieved the gun from the restaurant bar, then bundled him into their Police car and left without a word.

The epilogue is that the young man had escaped from an institution, and that when I had dialed 999 and asked for the Police, they were already looking for him in our area. This is why they reached us so quickly. We never knew where he had obtained the gun from, but the Police did confirm that it was real and loaded. We later received a letter from the Police in Salisbury, praising us for our prompt action that had resulted in the apprehension of a potentially dangerous person.

I relaid this to the customers in the restaurant later that evening and I'm quite sure that they did not believe me. We still have the letter from the Police. Incidentally, that was the only time that we called the police in twenty-two years at The Oak.

COLD AND DARK

The restaurant had only just started to attract a regular clientele when the three day week came into effect. The three day week was one of several measures introduced in the United Kingdom by the Conservative Government, to conserve electricity. Coal was a major source of energy for the production of electricity at the time and the coal miners were on strike at the same time as a global oil crisis. This lasted from January 1974 until March 7th. We could only open for three days a week with limited use of electricity. No external pub lighting, no backlights in the bar and little or no electric heating. Not the way to run a successful hospitality business. However, due to our youthful enthusiasm and a healthy local following, we survived.

THAT JACKDAW!

As trade gradually increased, space again became a limiting factor, so we decided to tidy up the back yard. This was the area between the pub kitchen and the restaurant. We decided to add tables and chairs to this area.

In order to keep staffing levels at a reasonable level, we decided not to provide table service, but to ask customers to order their food at the bar. When their food was ready, we called their name using a simple tannoy system. This worked well, but it was amazing how many Mr. Smiths were customers and how many partners some had!

One day a tame Jackdaw decided to become a regular visitor to the backyard area. He became a popular source of amusement, but also a costly problem as he acquired a taste for real ale. He would land on a customer's table shouting "Jack Jack" then plunge his head into their pint of beer, have a good swig then fly off spraying beer everywhere. The consequence was, although the other customers thought this was hilarious, I was regularly confronted by the one whose beer 'Jack' had sampled and thus contaminated, demanding a replacement pint. This situation lasted for several weeks, then suddenly 'Jack' disappeared. We will never know if he just decided to go elsewhere or customer quietly wrung his neck for sharing his beer!

That Jackdaw!

ANOTHER GUN?

For some years we had a Fruit Machine installed in the public bar. The early ones had the conventional fruit display (hence their name), that paid out a jackpot when a line of the same fruit came up. More sophisticated machines followed, and we had one that depicted an airplane flying across the screen. The objective was to shoot it down to obtain the jackpot. If you hit it there was a loud bang as the airplane exploded, followed by the clatter of coins.

One evening, one of the regulars who reckoned he had cracked the way to beat the machine and shoot the airplane, was feeding coins into it with great determination. He had about ten locals crowded closely around him in anticipation, when, BANG went the exploding airplane,

"Sh-t, I've been shot," cried the guy playing the machine and the crowd leapt back simultaneously, all mouthing interesting expletives!

Apparently, the machine had developed an electrical short circuit and when the airplane exploded had momentarily become 'live' The player and those touching him, had all received an electric shock. Thank goodness no one was seriously affected and the good result was that the chap playing the machine was almost cured from his love of fruit machines, despite the fact that he had won the jackpot!

In later years, as food became more and more popular, the noise from fruit machines did not fit our business profile. The various noises that they emitted annoyed some diners, and so they were removed. The brewery company was not too happy with this, as it had a share in fruit machine income throughout it's estate. But they turned a blind eye as beer and wine sales had increased considerably. Yet another commercial decision, unpopular with a minority.

THE CELLAR HATCH

The hatch to the cellar was always a hazard as it was situated at the end of the walkway behind the bar and was also just in front of the door from the pub kitchen. Often, during service it was necessary to go down to the cellar to change a barrel, and that meant there was a gaping hole in the floor behind the bar. One evening, I opened the hatch and without shouting the usual warning, I descended into the cellar. I was just about to ascend the small ladder back up to the bar, when there was a shriek and I was confronted with a very attractive pair of thighs, topped with a pair of scanty white knickers. Before I had a chance to fully appreciate this vision, a young lady was sitting on my head closely followed by a tray loaded with hot food! Fortunately, I came off worse than she did and we were able to laugh about it later. I think that both of our imaginations produced considerably more detail of this event than actually happened, as we gave each other very knowing looks when passing from then on! These days I would no doubt be sued for negligence, and for voyeurism.

HERBIE AND HIS NAVY TALES

Herbie, the ex-marine who was still in the bar guarding the till after the kitchen fire, generally didn't say much. However, one evening when I served him his tot of rum, he said,

"This reminds me of a time that I was in 'The Andrew', (an old term for The Royal Navy), I was staying in a barracks (that he referred to as a Brick Ship) in Portsmouth. I had been on a run ashore and arrived, very much the worse for wear, back to my cabin. I had half a bottle of rum with me, and after having one last drink before turning in decided to go to the head (toilet). To my disgust, I had closed the cabin door leaving the key outside and the door would not open. I was locked in. There was a window in the cabin, but even standing on a chair it was too high for me to pee from. The only receptacle that I had to pee in was my rum bottle and that was half full and I was already full of rum! However, nature was calling big time, so a decision had to be made. I could not waste the rum, so I drank it, peed in the bottle, emptied the bottle out of the window and collapsed!"

He was in full flow with his tales now and had gathered a small audience.

"Brickwoods," he said, "the local brewery, was running a competition to decide on a name for a new beer that they had brewed. They gave the Royal Marines, who were stationed in the local barracks some samples to try and requested that they give them their considered opinion. The representative for the brewery arrived a few days later to obtain the result of the Marines tasting experience. The Marine's opinion, as major consumers of their products, was important. He asked us what name we suggested. 'Love in a boat' was what we came up with. The rep asked why we called it that. It was because it was f-----g near water!'"

I remember one evening when Herbie had been sitting on a bar stool quietly drinking a pint of beer, when he just fell off the stool and lay still on the floor.

"Is he dead John?" I asked, very concerned.

"Ask him if a whisky would help," replied John knowingly.

I leaned over the bar and looked down at Herbie, who was not moving.

"Would a whisky help Herbie?" I asked.

Herbie nimbly climbed back onto his stool and said, "Oh thank you, a large one please."

OLD CUSTOMS

When you take over a pub, some old customs, and customers, inevitably come with it.

Dogs in pubs were one. There is, as usual, a story involved as well. A dear old couple named Tom and Ruby used to arrive every evening without fail at about eight pm. Apparently, they had spent their honeymoon at The Royal Oak.

They arrived on a little motor bike with a sidecar attached. Tom drove the motorbike, with Ruby, his wife, on the pillion seat, and Cleo the dog in the sidecar! Cleo was undoubtedly their 'baby'. Allegedly, once when Cleo had been unwell, Ruby had been seen regularly around Wilton, where they lived, pushing Cleo in a full sized children's pram with Cleo wrapped in a blanket wearing a little bonnet. They would come in, take off their biking gear, order a pint of bitter for Tom and half a pint of bitter for Ruby.

Tom was a connoisseur of the Ushers Best Bitter and would take a sip, swill it around his mouth, and announce very seriously when he reckoned the barrel had been tapped and how much beer had been used to date. To be fair, he was usually spot on. Cleo would then place her paws on the counter and Ruby would say to whoever was on the bar,

"She is asking for her cheese."

Traditionally, a square of cheese was delivered, and Tom and Ruby proceeded to give Cleo small pieces during the evening. We went along with this for a while but quickly put a stop to Cleo sharing Tom's beer from his pint mug. One regular, who was less tolerant, would wander in, select the stool that Cleo was perched on, swipe the little dog off with one swift blow, and plonk himself on the stool, muttering profanities.

Another couple would regularly bring two brown spaniels into the bar. They were usually well behaved, but occasionally would get excited and chase around the bar. Their owners seemed oblivious that this really was not ok. Darts were still being played at the time and I witnessed several darts being aimed at them when they dashed in front of the players. Fortunately the players were lousy shots.

The final straw came when a young lady entered the small lounge bar one evening. Accompanying her was a small poodle that promptly cocked its leg against a post in the middle of the bar. The lady watched this in amusement. Fortunately, I had seen it as well and without thinking shouted,

"Get that bloody dog out and don't ever bring it back!" I never saw either of them again.

As food was becoming more and more popular, dogs in the pub did not fit the profile and we said that, due to hygiene regulations, they were no longer allowed. Fortunately, no one seriously questioned this. Providing Cleo drank from an ashtray from then on and did not sit on a stool, we turned a blind eye to this little charade. After all, Cleo was not a dog, she was their 'baby'!

Cleo in the Sidecar

THE BIG EXPANSION

Towards the end of the seventies, trade had increased to such an extent that the buildings' facilities were inadequate. We had meaningful discussions with senior management with the brewery, which was our landlord, and in exchange for a realistic increase in our rent, it was agreed that substantial building work would take place.

The large garage, which was in poor shape, was demolished and rebuilt as a large storage area for frozen and dry goods. It was connected to the restaurant kitchen. The backyard was enclosed, and became part of the pub and the bar servery was extended. We undertook the decoration and fitting out, and the whole project took about six months to complete.

The rent for the pub increased every three years. A considerable increase in turnover was not supposed to be taken into consideration in the negotiation process. However, it was very apparent to us that it was, as each review resulted in a considerable proposed uplift.

Fortunately however, on a short break with the children to north Wales, we had purchased some land. My Dad had advised us to, "buy land, they've stopped making it". With the help of the local builders, we designed a bungalow on our land and had it built by local Welsh builders. This proved to be a great asset, particularly when the rent review process started. Most tenants had sold any property that they had owned, in order to raise the money to cover the up front expenses involved when they entered the trade. This meant that the only home that they now had was the pub that they rented. We had our own home, so if the proposed rent seemed excessive, we suggested that they find another tenant. This ploy worked for five rent reviews! Then it didn't.

Katie and Colin Fisher
and 'Team'
welcome you
to the

Royal Oak Inn

Great Wishford,
Near Salisbury,
Wilts.

The 'Inn' Restaurant Menu

Throughout the premises we offer the 'Inn Restaurant Menu' which ranges from a sandwich to a full three or four course Cordon Bleu meal – the choice is yours.

Tables may be booked in the main dining room, on Monday to Saturday evening – inclusive, where full waitress service is available at no extra cost.

This menu is available every lunchtime and evening.

Sunday lunchtimes a traditional roast is added.

We make every possible dish at the 'Oak' and bake bread daily.

All our meat, fruit and vegetables are supplied fresh from local suppliers.

Jams and Chutneys

We are probably one of the only pubs in the land 'licensed' to make and sell our own range of jams and chutneys. These are made with fruits in season' and are on display in the bars.

A selection from our extensive Menu:

Mussells, King Prawns, Whitebait, Clams, Sole, Salmon, Halibut, Trout.

Avocados, Melon, Pate, Prawns in Brandy, Prawn Mayonnaise, Prawn Cocktail.

Fillet, T. Bone and Rump Steaks plus delicious Wine Sauces, Duckling, Veal, Pork, Game, Chicken.

A selection of Hot Pies with a choice of ten fillings.
Chilli Con Carne, Curry, Lasagne, Moussaka.
A selection of Vegetarian Dishes.

Treacle Roly Poly, Bread and Butter Pudding, Fruit Crumbles, Fresh Fruit Parfaits, Profiteroles, Meringues, Brandy Snaps, Ice Cream Sundaes, Cream Gateaux.

Wines

We stock a comprehensive list of wines including country wines and English wine from Kent.

On Draught

Ushers' Best Bitter and Founders Ale – from the pump! Ushers' Country Bitter, Ben Truman, Triple Crown Bitter, Carlsberg and Fosters Lager, Guinness, Ciders and Milk!

Ice Cream and Sorbets

All of our ice creams are made with fresh cream and eggs and the sorbets are made using fresh fruits.

Catering Facilities

We are able to cater for parties of up to 100 people. Please ask for quotations for that special occasions – wedding – or just anything.

We are in lots of guides but value your opinions and suggestions most of all!

The Expansion Begins

Kate, Colin, and Jacky

THIS STILL HURTS

As anyone in business will appreciate, expanding the business also increases the logistical problems, the main one being the necessary increase in the number of staff required. We needed to employ more bar staff, more cooks, more people for prepping meals, and a number of cleaners and pot men or women.

We also believed in training staff at all levels, and as Kate and I physically couldn't do everything, we relied on staff who had been with us for some time to help with this. This generally worked well, until one evening we had left two young trainee barmen, under the guidance of a middle aged man who had worked for us as a barman for several years. He was very popular and extremely efficient, and an obvious choice as a trainer.

We had gone to visit my brother, who lived in Salisbury, and didn't expect to be back until just after closing time. However, we returned just before closing time. Our trusted trainer was smoking a large cigar and drinking a large whisky whilst the two young trainees were both enjoying scampi and chips together with a glass of wine. I was astounded, and took the man aside.

"I'm really disappointed in you. You are fired. Please leave." I then turned to the two young lads who were looking very sheepish.

"You do realise, I suppose, that this practice is not allowed. What did your trainer say to you?"

"He said that while you were away, let's enjoy ourselves, they can afford it," he replied.

The trainer had sent a food order to the kitchen in the usual manner, but not for a customer!

We kept both of these lads on and they stayed faithfully with us for several years.

This had really upset us, as the man concerned had been someone that we had known for ages and really trusted. However, it was another lesson in running a successful business. It prompted strict stock control, pricing structures and cash management from then on.

We only had an old cash register at the time. One that I had purchased at auction and put stickers over the original pound shilling and pence symbols to convert it to decimal. The conversions were 'near enough'! During the upgrade of the pub, three new cash registers were installed, one in the restaurant and two in the bars. These enabled much tighter control and identified what transactions each staff member had made. Each staff member had a personal code and it was a case for dismissal if these codes were swapped. Also, we could now see exactly what product had been sold and by whom. This is all common practice now, but was pretty revolutionary then.

I then produced a stock record and ordering system. An overall stock level was agreed and then topped up on an "order up to" system every week. Every menu item had a recipe with individual product cost, gross profit margin (VAT), and suggested selling price. This took ages to accomplish, but once in place was simple to keep up to date and the cooks could use it when implementing new dishes. A similar book controlled the profit margin and pricing structure for wet sales. Cigarettes were high cost, low margin and were kept on a shelf behind the bar. I reckoned these were being stolen, but I couldn't figure out how. I made a drawing of the cigarette profile, thinking that if some disappeared, at least I could determine which ones were missing. After a while, we decided that he or she who was pinching the cigarettes had twigged my plan, so took a packet from each pile thus keeping the profile the same!

We had cigarette machines installed as although the profit margins were extremely small using them, none were getting stolen.

We had learned another lesson as our business expanded. Running a cash oriented business created some tempting circumstances and it was our responsibility to take appropriate precautions.

THE ANNUAL FIRE

Although we had it swept regularly, once a year, without fail, the chimney in the public bar caught fire. We even had a special liner installed, as originally oak beams actually crossed the chimney space halfway up so it's a wonder that the pub hadn't burned to the ground years before.

The local fire brigade were a part time, happy go lucky bunch, and many were regulars. They had a well practiced routine when attending our chimney fires. Some came into the bar with floor covering and buckets to take away debris, others climbed onto the roof to hose a fine spray of water down the chimney, while the remainder got the drinks in!

Our staff knew most of them and had witnessed at least one chimney fire, so also knew what each fireman liked to drink. By the time that the fire had been extinguished, the appropriate drinks were lined up along the counter. The firemen stayed for the rest of the evening on the pretence of ensuring that the fire was completely extinguished, but mostly for the free drinks. One of the old firemen said that he was soon to retire and would miss his annual trip to The Oak and the free drinks.

THE WALKING STICK

A very pleasant chap named Lenny used to come in now and again. He had been a submariner and apparently had survived being depth charged during the war. This left him with shell shock symptoms that caused him to walk wobbly and shake a lot. Initially, I thought that he was inebriated, but was soon put in the picture by John. He always walked, as he was unable to drive, from close to Wilton, where he lived. One evening after closing time, I was just checking the toilets on my routine to ensure that no one was in there and everywhere else was secure, when there in the gents toilet was Lenny flat on his back still holding his 'John Thomas'.

"I fell over and can't get up," he said, very seriously. I helped him up and sat him on a chair. Wanting to get him on his way, I asked him if he could walk.

"Not without a walking stick," he announced.

I found a walking stick that belonged to one of the fishermen and said,

"Here you are Lenny, now you can get going."

He took a long look at the walking stick and shook his head.

"I can't use that," he replied, after a long pause.

"Why on earth not," I said, losing patience.

"Because it's not oak," he replied.

"Bollocks!" Was my answer to that.

I had had enough of this so dragged him outside and into my car. Then I drove him to his home. At opening time the next morning, there was Lenny with a bunch of flowers for Kate and a box of chocolates for me. Bless him.

KERRY

We always had an advert in the pub for bar staff as there was a natural turnover of students. One day a big man with a bushy black beard came in and said that he was looking for evening work and was available any evening. His name was Kerry. He had a charming smile and when he told me he was ex-Royal Navy, we had something in common, so I employed him. Kerry very soon became extremely popular with the customers, and was very efficient behind the bar. He was a star at waiting tables in the restaurant too. Despite his size, he managed to nimbly work his way around the tables all the time interacting happily with the customers.

Kerry was large. While in the Navy he had regularly boxed for the Navy at light heavyweight. One evening, in Portsmouth he had been run over by a car and very seriously injured. As a result of his injuries, his weight became a problem and involved regular hormone implants. Consequently, he was invalided out of the Navy. He lived about three miles away near Langford and insisted on walking to and from work, regardless of the weather or time, as he considered that he needed the exercise.

There was an awkward customer who regularly came on a saturday evening and insisted on sitting in front of the bar, in the narrowest part of the bar, thus making it very difficult for other customers to get by. One evening, after being asked politely to move to no avail, Kerry winked at me.

"No worries, Boss, just watch," he whispered to me.

He walked up to the offending customer and without saying a word lifted him, still on his chair, and carried him over the heads of other customers and deposited him further along the bar out of the way. He then continued to collect empty glasses as if nothing had happened.

Members of staff like Kerry are gems, particularly in the hospitality trade where charisma is so important, and cannot be taught. He became our best trainer and worked most evenings.

One day, Kerry took Kate aside and asked her to look at his implant site, as it was painful. Kate, being an ex-nurse, efficiently examined the wound, and carefully dressed it. She advised him to see his doctor the next day. He did and was immediately admitted to hospital. We visited two days later and gave him some bottles of Guinness, his favourite tipple. He was his usual jovial self and was confident that he would soon be back at work. Five days later, Kerry died of septicemia. We closed the pub and nearly every member of staff and many customers attended his funeral. Rest in peace good friend.

CELEBRITY VISITS

Many celebrities came through our doors, but nearly all wished to remain anonymous. On one occasion a famous footballer, Jack Charlton, and a few friends came in. Jack Charlton was a famous English footballer and manager. He was in the English team that won the World Cup in 1966. He managed the Republic of Ireland national team from 1986-1996, achieving two World Cups and one European Championship.

Although he gave his name quietly when ordering food, one of the old locals, called Alf, recognised him immediately. He was so excited he almost leapt upon him.

"Jack, you have given us so much pleasure, gosh it's so good to meet you, look who's here lads."

Jack was all smiles and very polite. By the afternoon old Alf had written to all of his family and his grandchildren. He talked about that meeting for the rest of his life.

On another occasion the restaurant area had been booked for a small private party with snacks and champagne. A very smart lady came in early that morning, and told us that the party consisted of a famous film actor who wanted to keep a low profile and that he would like us to be discreet. He duly arrived in a white limousine and was whisked into the restaurant. To this day, I haven't a clue who he was!

THE SURVIVORS

Early one evening, I was working at the bar, when two fit young men came in and ordered a couple of beers and wanted to know what food was available. We looked at each other and simultaneously said,

"I recognise you."

While I was in the Royal Navy at Britannia Royal Naval College, there were two quite challenging exercises. One was a PLX (Patrol Leadership Exercise) and the other a ten day survival course. I had endured both of these as a Cadet at the college and these men were the physical training instructors at that time. Both of these courses took place on Dartmoor. The Royal Naval College is situated in Devon, and Dartmoor is a rugged national park covering three hundred and sixty eight square miles, closeby.

"What the devil are you guys doing here?" I enquired.

"Well, Dartmoor and the New Forest are out of bounds for our exercises at present due to foot and mouth disease, so we are using Grovely Wood instead. We have twenty Navy cadets in the woods already and they have to survive for ten days. We are there to guide them, help them catch food, and generally stay alive.

When I was on the escape and evasion survival course on Dartmoor, one of the cadet's parents in my team owned a small hotel on the moor. We evaded capture long enough to reach the hotel where we stayed for several days whilst lying low. Royal Marines were engaged to represent an enemy, catch the cadets and endeavour to interrogate them, not too gently! Residents in the area were to be regarded as enemies and had been advised not to help us, but the Hotel for some reason had been excluded.

When it was about time to surface, we were given a lift in the Hotel's minibus and were dropped off a couple of miles away from the Royal Naval College. Fortunately it was pouring with rain at the time so by the time we reached the college we looked suitably muddy and disheveled. That *is* survival isn't it?

Anyway, the next evening, the two instructors came in again and I handed over the bar service to John.

"I'm just popping out for a while," I explained.

I drove up the road at the back of the pub to Grovely Wood. It's a big wood and a bit of a maze up there, but I knew it well and soon found the bunch of Navy cadets gathered around a fire. It didn't take long for me to explain who I was and that I had also been to Dartmouth and quite understood their predicament. We came to a mutually satisfactory arrangement. Each evening, I would leave a big bag of victuals for them, hidden in a bush by the railway bridge, situated behind the pub. This situation worked a treat. Every evening, the instructors came in. They had a meal, and often stayed drinking until closing time. The bag of victuals was carefully collected each evening while the instructors were otherwise engaged. The instructors did announce during the end of the ten days that the group of cadets on the course were one of the best that they had ever experienced and appeared to thrive on minimal food.

About three weeks later we had a letter with the names of all of the Royal Navy Cadets involved and a cheque that more than covered the food that we had supplied. I wonder to this day if those instructors really knew what was going on, and indeed, when I had been at Dartmouth, did they know about the hotel?

SOME OF THE REGULARS

Old Joe was a great character. He had somehow damaged his back badly and due to the ensuing arthritis, was permanently bent almost double. As he entered the bar, several locals would say in unison,

"Here comes Jo, here's his head, his ass is coming!"

Great Wishford had a railway station up until 1955, and Joe had been the station master for many years. As trains puffed to a stop at the railway station he would call through the tannoy system,

"Wishford, Wishford, this is Wishford."

When the station closed, Joe was relocated to Salisbury railway station. He was well remembered for his regular memory lapses when calling out the station's name. Apparently, he regularly called out,

"Wishford, Wishford, nay bugger tis Salisbury."

Another regular was the vicar from a nearby village. He was a real character and would often dash in early on a Sunday morning before opening time, breathlessly announcing that he had drunk all of the altar wine and needed a couple of bottles of cheap sherry to tide him over. He was quite charming, and had some affliction that caused him to shake and twitch all of the time. Apparently, he had always been like that, but had become an army chaplain during the war and had seen action in France. He was renowned for going onto the battlefield to give the last rites to dying soldiers. His theory was that there was no such thing as an atheist on a battlefield and he wasn't in the slightest concerned about what side the wounded were on. He often strayed right into the enemy lines. Consequently he was captured by the Germans. Allegedly, he became such a nuisance to them, that they sent him back! I can't verify this, but was assured that it was true, and knowing him, I can quite believe it.

BRITISH LEYLAND

In 1982, The Austin Ambassador car was launched by the Austin Rover Group subsidiary of British Leyland. Using the same body shell, it was offered in two engine sizes, 1.7 litres or 2.00 litres. The National press had been invited to test drive the new cars, and we had been chosen as a pit stop, potty break stop, and change car venue. Three of each vehicle arrived ready for the press, who were coming from Bournemouth to have refreshments and change cars for trials over designated routes. Six cars arrived, each with four members of the press. They were a great bunch of young men and women and soon demolished big piles of sandwiches and cakes.

Suddenly, there was a hush. Someone was receiving a news flash on his radio. Without a word the room emptied and they rushed into all but three of the test cars and dissapeared. It transpired that The Laker Airline had just announced bankruptcy. This obviously was a bigger story than the new Ambassador, hence the sudden departure of the press.

Freddie Laker was a British entrepreneur who started a budget Trans-Atlantic airline in 1977. This proved to be very successful, but rival, larger airlines, clubbed together and set up similar budget fares. This competition proved to be too much, and eventually Laker Airlines folded.

I felt sorry for British Leyland, as they had put a lot of effort into the launch. However, I spent the next few hours testing both models. Funny enough, while talking to one of the journalists, I mentioned that I had started writing this book. She gave me her card and said that as soon as it was finished to call her and she would help to get it published. Needless to say, I have lost her card and have no recollection of her name. That was nearly forty years ago, though.

ONE MAN'S MEAT

When you undertake a fairly extensive food and drink operation, inevitably you attract food and drink aficionados, or rather folk who reckon that they are! Diners become food critics and drinkers, connoisseurs of real ale. Not a bad situation, as it keeps you on the ball. One very busy Sunday lunchtime, when we were packed out and hard pressed to cope, a steak was sent back to the kitchen. The server advised that the customer said that it was too tough to eat. The customer had not actually tasted it, but had come to this conclusion by cutting into it. We cooked another steak, and remembering some friends who ran a steakhouse, made sure that it went out with a razor sharp knife. Their theory was that you rarely had a complaint of a steak being tough if your knives were razor sharp.

However, within minutes of being served, back it came. Once again too tough to eat! The customer had just cut the steak and not tried it.

"I'll go and see him," I told the embarrassed server.

"I'm sorry sir, we don't seem to be able to please you with our steaks," I said, being somewhat exasperated.

"It's too tough to eat, and I know my steaks, young man!" He replied.

"It is actually very tender sir, I tried it before it came out," I added.

"Nonsense, you obviously don't know that it can't possibly be tender, it's pink in the middle," he said very pompously.

"You ordered it cooked medium, and that *is* medium," I said, now becoming irate.

"Medium means cooked right through young man, for goodness sake, I know what I ordered!" He countered.

We cooked the steak until it was 'well done' and delivered it to the customer once more. As he left the pub, he advised the server that we had eventually cooked his steak properly.

"I hope that your chef has learned something." he added smugly..

He was correct about that, we had learned something: awkward buggers come with this business!

A DAY'S WORK

Having three residents and one bathroom, with no hot and cold facilities in the bedrooms, required some strategic planning at times. Breakfast, and the early morning routine, when the fishermen were in residence, was such a case.

One of the fishermen was served tea in bed at 8 AM, the next at 8.30 AM and the last one at 9 AM. That enabled them to get up and ablute in an orderly fashion. Breakfast then proceeded at half hour intervals, with little conversion, and indeed, little sign of recognition during this ritual. This little routine usually took until about 11 AM, when their 'work day' began. Fishing was the work of the day and taken very seriously. They discussed which beat they each would take. It was a rule of the Wilton Fly Fishing Club that members kept well away from one another, and only fished dry fly upstream. They normally returned between 3 PM and 4 PM in the afternoon, to adjourn to the Lounge Bar, compare notes, and enjoy their favorite tipple. They were very unselfish, and would share their knowledge of a decent trout's whereabouts, and would be genuinely pleased if any one of them caught one of these. One afternoon they had invited a retired Colonel, also a member of the fishing club, for pre-dinner drinks, and he informed them that he had spotted a whopper earlier that day.

"Where was it?" Enquired Mr. Roughead.

"Oh, I couldn't divulge that." Replied the Colonel, somewhat pompously.

"What strange company you must keep," admonished Mr. Roughead meaningfully.

A Days Work

THE CHIPPERFIELDS

The famous Chipperfield Circus has links to Great Wishford. Richard Chipperfield, one of the earlier members of the family, moved his wagon to the field just past the railway bridge, behind The Royal Oak, and this was his base until he died in 1959. He is buried in St. Giles graveyard along with other members of the Chipperfield family.

We had the privilege of meeting some of them as family funerals are still held in Great Wishford, and several were held there during our time at The Royal Oak. They were always charming, and came into the pub for refreshment, but always maintained the circus tradition of not drinking alcohol, or smoking.

When there was a Chipperfield funeral, the grave was adorned with the most amazing flower arrangements, sometimes depicting huge displays of flowers in the shape of animals associated with the circus.

A GOOD READ!

In an endeavour to make a visit to "The Oak" more than somewhere to eat, drink and be merry, we wrote little quotations, on blackboards situated in both bars. These were sourced from stories of old inns. Here are a few of them:

'And still the wonder grew,
That one small head could carry all he knew.' -Unknown

'Damn their eyes,
If ever they tries,
To keep a poor man,
From his beer.' -Unknown

'But first quad he,
her at this ale stake,
I will bothe drynke and byten on a cake,' -Chaucer

Long poles, or Stakes, indicated an Ale house in middle English times.

'His arguments in silly circles run,
Still round and round, and end where they begun.
So the poor turnspit, as the wheel runs round,
The more he gains, the more he loses ground...' -Unknown

Turn spits were used to turn the meat as it cooked over a fire. Dogs were trained to run around the wheel.

"Does the convict love his crank and treadmill, or the galley slave his oar or bench?"-Unknown

"John Adams lies here, of the parish of Southwell,
A Carrier who carried his can to his mouth well,

He carried so much and he carried so fast,
He could carry no more-so was carried at last;
For the liquor he drank, being too much for one,
He could not carry off, so now is carri-on." -Byron

"Let me have men about me that are fat:
Sleek-headed men, and such as sleep o' nights,
Yond Cassius has a lean and hungry look:
He thinks too much: such men are dangerous." -Shakespeare

"And when the bottle at last grows old,
And will good liquor no longer hold,
Out of its sides you may make a clout to mend your shoes when they're worn out,
Or take and hang upon a pin,
Twill serve to put hinges and odd things in.
So I hope his soul in Heaven may dwell,
Who first found out the Leather Bottle!" -Unknown

"O would I were where I would be!
There would I be where I am not;
For where I am would I not be,
And where I would be I can not." -Unknown

There were many more.

IT'S THE WAY WE SAY IT

We had employed a very well spoken young lady to help in the bar. One morning I heard her shriek with laughter and went to investigate.

"What's so funny?" I asked.

"This young man asked me if we sold poison here," she replied, still chuckling.

"I never did," said the young man, "I said, do you sell poise in 'ere."

"It's just our Wiltshire pronunciation," I explained. "What he means is, 'do we sell pies in here?'"

Another misunderstanding happened soon after my Dad had given our children two ducklings. They were very tame and sometimes wandered into the kitchen demanding food. One day, one of them decided to fly, and disappeared over the pub towards the village. I went up the road, and there was a new resident to the village leaning on his gate.

"Good morning," I said, "I've lost my white duck (pronounced 'dug'), have you seen him?"

"No," he replied, "but I'll look out for him, which way did he go?"

"He flew over the pub, over your garden, going this way, I think," I replied.

Later that day a local came in and said, "That new bloke up the road is worried about you, Col."

"Why?" I asked.

"He said that you were looking for your white dog this morning, and you told him it had flown over the pub!"

One of our locals worked on one of the farms in the area and would often greet me in the morning with, "Whey Up!".

Even though I had been born and bred in Wiltshire, I had not heard this expression. When I asked the farmer that he worked for what it meant, he chuckled and replied,

"It means 'good morning', 'nice day isn't it?', or anything else you want it to mean. These farm lads don't say much!"

A SERIES OF THEFTS

Back in the seventies and eighties almost every transaction was in cash, so to see a till bulging with notes could be a very tempting sight. Three occasions caused us to implement controls that were used in managed houses where any discrepancies involving cash or stock, became contractual issues with the relevant pub company.

Staff were advised of the following rules designed to protect us and them:

1. No cash was to be brought to work. On that basis, any cash found on a member of staff would be considered to be stolen.
2. Any bags brought to work had to be put in the male or female lockers. It was recognised that female staff required personal items.
3. When using the tills, personal codes were required before each transaction and 'No sales' needed explaining on the till roll.
4. No alcohol was to be consumed when working. Customers often offered to buy staff drinks. Staff should politely advise that they were not allowed to drink on duty, but could ring the offered amount in the till for later)
5. Staff were made aware that close friends or family were not discouraged but should not get discounted prices.

This simple set of rules was explained to every new staff member and they had to sign that they had seen it, and were given a copy for retention.

During our time at The Oak, we had purchased some land in North Wales. This became our refuge from the stress of 'Living on The Job'.

On our regular trips to North Wales we became friends with a talented Welsh potter. His products included a variety of jars, pots, jugs, and mugs, all being original designs, fired in his old wood-fueled kiln.

We loved his products and sold them in the pub. Kate and I dealt with these sales, and kept the cash in a vase in our lounge. We paid the potter cash, and our margin was a perk!

One day, Kate called me aside.

"Have you taken any money from the vase?" She asked.

"No, why?" I replied.

"Fifty pounds are missing." She replied.

"Oh, bugger, we have a thief," I said, "but who?"

"Only one of the cleaners should come in here, and she is still here." Kate said quietly, "Let's get her in."

We called the young girl in.

"There is cash missing from that vase, do you know anything about it," I asked her sternly.

She went very red and burst out crying.

"No I don't, what a nasty thing to say," she sobbed.

"I think she is lying," said Kate, "her mother is in the kitchen, I'll go and get her and explain the situation, keep the girl here."

Kate returned with a very irate mother. She confronted her daughter.

"Don't mess with me, have you taken that money?" She shouted.

"No," she said quietly.

Kate then said, "I think that we should call the Police straight away as I'm sure she is lying. They will send a police woman who will search her."

"I'll search her!" Said the mother, "leave the room, please Colin".

Kate was correct. Fifty pounds were found tucked in her knickers. We didn't call the police, as this would have resulted in that young girl having a criminal record. The mother was understandably very embarrassed, but we all agreed to learn from the experience and move on. No one was dismissed on this occasion.

The next time we had money missing was after a particularly busy Saturday evening.

We had to constantly top the change up in the tills. The routine was that we kept a bag with 100 pounds in change in the room behind the bar. It was out of sight of customers, but no secret to staff. When five pounds, in change, was removed from the bag and added to the till, it was replaced with a five pound note, so the bag should always hold 100 pounds.

The next morning, before checking the tills and sorting out the floats for that day, I had taken a bag of rubbish to the rubbish bay behind the pub and noticed the change bag under another rubbish bag. I took it back to the office and there was 60 pounds, not 100 pounds in the bag.

What was it doing in the rubbish bay and where was the other 40 pounds?

Another thief!

We questioned everyone who had worked that evening and narrowed it down to the only one who had been tasked to take rubbish from the kitchen to the rubbish bay. It was a young girl from the village.

I telephoned the young girl's mother and quietly explained the situation, and that it looked very likely that her daughter had stolen some cash.

"Nonsense," she yelled at me, "I have always brought my children up to be honest."

"Please just talk to her and call me back, as we are about to call the police." I said.

She didn't answer and slammed the phone down. A natural reaction when someone accuses their child of stealing.

Less than ten minutes later she called me back to say that she has questioned her daughter and she knows nothing about the money.

"Well," I replied, "We have found the bag that held the missing money and we will hand it to the Police. It will have the fingerprints of the culprit on it, so we will soon know the truth."

This was a bit tongue in cheek, but did the trick.

Five minutes later she called me back.

"I don't know what to say," she sobbed, I've just searched her room and found forty pounds in change in four plastic bags."

"I'm on the way to you now with the money, and the girl."

The mother and daughter duly arrived.

The mother pushed the girl towards me screaming, "You don't belong to me, you are going into a home!"

The poor girl was sobbing uncontrollably, but handed me the money.

"How were you going to collect the rest of the cash left in the rubbish bay?" I asked her.

"I don't know what you mean." she answered. Maybe she had not considered that! We will never know.

We advised all of the staff that had worked that evening that the culprit had been caught quite quickly. It was a lesson to all of them that we did check the cash situation carefully. It was a lesson to us as well and the tills and change were checked in the evenings from then on, before the staff had finished. Once again, we did not call the police and have a young girl lumbered with a record. The young girl resigned!

NOW IT'S STOCK!

We sold a huge number of puddings and deserts, and several dishes involved the use of chocolate flakes. However, I thought that we were using far more than the number of servings that required them. It seemed that one, or maybe several members of staff, had a sweet tooth! Eager to find the culprit, I drilled a hole in the ceiling of the storeroom, above the shelving that held the boxes of flakes. We bribed Nick, our son, and Jacky, our daughter, to position themselves in the loft, each armed with drinks, biscuits, a torch, pens, and a notebook. They stayed there one Sunday lunchtime session from just before the staff arrived until just after they left. Some three hours. We considered that to catch the culprit(s) would take a week of observation. Our spy children observed three members of staff during that first session eat flakes on trips to the storeroom. A total of eighteen flakes that period.

"I'm not doing that again! I'm covered in fibreglass insulation, itch like hell, and am bursting for a pee," Nick complained.

"Nor am I," announced Jacky firmly.

There was a big cupboard in the storeroom so I drilled a hole in the door, and this was to be our lookout for the rest of the week. It was my turn next. Perched on a stool, in the cupboard, notebook in hand, I clocked two members of staff, who ate seven flakes in one session between them. Over the course of a week 144 chocolate flakes had been eaten by staff.

Apart from one adult, none of the main staff were involved. They were all youngsters who probably had never seen so much chocolate in their lives and the temptation was just too much. The funny thing was that we had a stock system in place for dry and frozen goods. When stock levels went too low, a form was filled in to order more. The missing flakes meant the stock level had gone below the order more level so the blighters had ordered more!

This was a tricky one to deal with. The senior member of staff had been seen to eat eleven flakes in one session. She was confronted, owned up and decided to resign. The youngsters were cautioned and remained on the payroll. Until now, no one knew how we knew!

Another interesting outcome was that I had put some very hot chilli powder in some flakes at the top of a box hoping the culprit would be easy to spot having eaten one. These were consumed with no obvious signs of discomfort.

Regrettably, from then on we had to implement even more systems for cash and stock control, on the premise that all staff were liable to be tempted. When we left "The Oak" and I was involved in the licensed trade ranging from small pubs to huge managed houses, restaurants and hotels, it was quite normal for most stockrooms, cellars and even tills in bars to be protected by CCTV.

TWO WEDDINGS

During our time at "The Oak", we catered for numerous wedding receptions. Two stand out, one, a very up market occasion during the summer. The groom to be was very precise with his requirements. Medium rare cold roast beef, a variety of fresh salads, and local new potatoes. For desert, lemon soufflè. Champagne, I can't remember the brand, ad lib, throughout the proceedings.

There were fifty guests, and this number necessitated a whole loin of beef being roasted to the desired "medium rare". This was a big joint of beef for us to manage, so we engaged a commercial caterer from Bournemouth to cook the beef for us. We also required more champagne glasses. We employed our best staff, rehearsed our roles several times, and waited that morning for the beef to be delivered.

Kate worried over the soufflé, as fifty was a challenge. To our relief, the beef arrived on time and was absolutely perfect. Our rehearsals had paid off and the whole reception went exactly according to plan.

In contrast, we catered for a different level of reception for a charming young local couple. They wanted fried chicken and chips followed by chocolate brownies and ice cream. A few bottles of wine on the tables and a free bar with a fixed budget. This worked perfectly and they had a great time.

After some rather ribald speeches they wandered around outside onto the small lawned area and we left them to it. I was quite concerned later, when checking to make sure everyone was happy, I found both the bride and groom laid side by side, on the lawn, totally paralytic!

"Oh dear," I exclaimed to the best man. "Is there anything we should do?"

"No, mate," he said. "They wouldn't reckon that this had been a success if they hadn't ended up like this. They are like this every Saturday night." Their theory is that if you can remember a good night out, it was not a really good night.

"Don't worry, they will sober up, stagger home, and be fine. I'll look after them."

THE GIRLS GO FISHING

Jacky, who was about ten years old at the time, and her cousin, Sarah, of the same age, wanted to go fishing. We thought that they could come to no harm, or do no harm, so I armed them both with a bamboo cane with about ten feet of string, a bent pin through a knot at the end. They managed to find a worm each and headed off to the river situated about 150 yards down the Langford road.

A couple of hours later there was a commotion in the bar and I went to investigate.

To everyone's amazement, the two monsters came back with a decent sized trout.

"What have you got there?" I said with a big grin.

"I think it's a trout Dad," said Jacky, "but we met Mr. Wrey on the way back from the river and he called it 'The bloody limit!'"

They confessed later that they did not catch the trout, Mr. Wrey had spotted them trying to catch one and had given them one that he had just caught. He told them to pretend that they had caught it. The ploy worked!

Mr. Roughead had also been fishing that day, and on his way to the river had met one of the local young ladies pushing a pram containing her new born baby.

"Let me see him?" requested Mr. Roughead.

"What a lovely baby," he announced. "Pity about it's wooden legs," he added chuckling, and wandered off.

The young lady wondered what on earth he meant and looked into the pram. She had collected some garden shears for her husband. The blades were hidden under the blankets and just the baby's head and the wooden handles were visible!

NICK ROUGHEAD CHECKS OUT

Nick Roughead died in 1975. Although he travelled the world and lived in serviced apartments, Albany, London, his affinity with Great Wishford was such that he is buried in the graveyard of St. Giles, just behind The Oak. His funeral also brings back memories. We catered for friends and a few family members, in the restaurant. One gentleman was very tearful and wandered round mumbling "Poor old Nick". Drinks were flowing freely and this chap enjoyed several very large whiskies.

Mr. Roughead's sister asked me if he was a friend of her brother, from the village.

"I have never seen him before." I replied.

Later that day, I related this to one of the locals. He laughed and said

"That's old Ted, he loves going to local funerals. He certainly did not know Nick Roughead, he just wanted a free drink!"

Later, I went to the cemetery for the service, accompanied by several customers.

One was a chap called Rip Kirby. He was a retired heavy forestry machinery engineer, who came in for a drink most lunchtimes. Apparently, some of the workers that he was associated with in the logging industry were extremely basic. To emphasise this, Rip advised that "some of them would put their dick where he wouldn't put his muddy gumboot".

He was renowned for taking food orders for the many elderly folk that frequented the bar at lunchtime. Then he delivered their meal as if employed as a waiter, which he wasn't! The customers loved him and he certainly added some character to the morning sessions. They often tipped him too!

While we were standing in the cemetery by the newly dug grave, one of the local lads turned to Rip and said,

"How old are you Rip?"

"I'm eighty nine," he replied.

"Hardly worth going home is it?" The young lad remarked dryly.

A memorable day for many reasons.

Dr. Bell died in 1970. It wasn't until after his death that we realised, that apart from being a very famous consultant Physician, he had been an accomplished artist with paintings exhibited in the Royal Academy, in London.

Chris Wrey died in 1976. It was not until after these three gentlemen had passed away that we realised how remarkable they all were. Each one of them had led an amazing life. They were the most charming, unassuming characters one could meet. It was our privilege to have played a small part, as a family, in their final years.

MORE RESIDENTS?

After the 'Fishermen' had all passed away, although we still offered accommodation to guests, we rarely had any! Quite a lot of people asked if we had any rooms available, but I hardly ever said yes. Kate would often ask why. My usual reply was that I didn't like the look of them. In all honesty, the facilities in the pub were basic, and with two young children, I was not comfortable with strangers being in the private quarters. The fishermen were a bit like family and had been roughing it at The Oak for years.

However, we did accept a booking for two nights for Lord and Lady P (unnamed). They duly arrived on a Friday evening, in an old Bentley. They settled themselves in their room and Lady P arranged her silver framed family photos above the fireplace and carefully laid out their medications on the table. We had installed hot and cold facilities in the rooms for the fishermen, but the bathroom and toilet were still shared with us.

When they had booked their dates, none of us had realised that they had booked on a bank holiday weekend. Consequently, we were extremely busy, and their quiet weekend in a secluded country inn was not quite as they had envisaged. They were charming, and presumably not used to really fancy accommodation. They were from a time where, although their castle was probably falling into disrepair and leaking like a sieve, they still retained a few faithful servants. This was quite apparent as they regularly called for tea, snacks, and drinks, to be served in the residents lounge, never once venturing into the bar.

The only request that rankled, was on the Sunday morning before they left, I was busy stocking the bar following a hectic Saturday evenings trade, when old Lord P leaned over the bar and said,

"Please could you have my car washed and polished before we leave?"

Bugger, I thought, *can't he see that I'm busy?*

Anyway, somehow I managed it, and off they went. They wrote a lovely note in the little guest book, saying how they had enjoyed their stay, but hadn't anticipated that we would be so busy. I wish we had kept their card, as we can't remember where they came from.

ANOTHER CHANGE

For several years we ran two kitchens, one for the restaurant, and one for the bars. This involved two menus. The restaurant had a more sophisticated menu, whereas the pub menu was simple. This worked very well, but after a few years, as pub food became more popular, it became apparent that yet another change was required to match the trend. Consequently, we decided to amalgamate the menus and offer the same menu throughout. The restaurant kitchen became the preparation kitchen, with the pub kitchen, having been upgraded, becoming the main hub. We continued to take bookings in the restaurant area.

Pub opening hours were restricted by law. However, we became so busy at weekends that we flouted these restrictions in order to cope. On a Saturday evening, by 6 PM, the car park was full, so we opened at 5.30 PM and sometimes even earlier to avoid the kitchen being overrun. Similarly, on Sunday lunchtimes, by 12 noon (the official opening time), we were so busy that we started opening at 11 AM.

On special occasions, such as Mother's Day, we ignored the law totally and stayed open until everyone had been served. Being out in "the sticks", the Police left us alone. At our peak, in the mid eighties, we averaged over two thousand meals a week, not counting sandwiches. We actually stopped serving sandwiches in the evening as they took as much time to prepare as a hot meal.

UP SELLING

Wastage in any catering establishment must be kept to a minimum. We bought 'par' baked frozen french bread rolls and baked batches as needed. However, on Saturday's we baked large numbers in advance, as ovens were being used for main courses. In order to ensure that these were all sold on Saturday evenings, we had a competition. The member of staff who sold the most rolls as 'garlic bread', at 50c each, received a bonus of 5 pounds. This worked so well that at times we had to bake more!

Another selling ploy on Saturday evenings was that I would sell pink champagne by the glass. If a man came in with a lady I would encourage him to buy her a glass of champagne. If he declined I would tell her that he didn't love her! Invariably, this worked, and as it was done in a playful manner we sold lots of champagne.

Country wines were also a great success. We sold them by the schooner. I made a huge plywood sign shaped like a schooner, and listed all the flavours available of it. These included, Cherry, Orange, Redcurrant, Whitecurrant, Raspberry, Mead, Peach, Blackberry, and Tangerine. We sold them by the bottle as well, and had our own labels printed. We purchased so much wine from our suppliers, that they supplied our house red and white wines already labelled with our name.

QUIET TIMES

Trade dropped off during the winter months. In order to retain our core staff during the quiet period, we decided to make jams and chutneys for sale in the bar for 'take away'. We became licensed jam and chutney manufacturers. I had to purchase jam jars in such quantities that it became necessary to purchase a small shed in order to store them. We also made ice cream, sorbets, and paté for the take away menu. These projects successfully kept staff employed. These ventures also involved regular visits from the health inspector to check our sterilization procedures for jam jars and bacteria tests on our Carpigiani ice cream machine.

Katie's Country Inn Foods

| LEMON MARMALADE |

Hand Made at
THE ROYAL OAK INN, GT. WISHFORD, SALISBURY, WILTS.

Ingredients.

Net Weight :

Katie's Country Inn Foods

ICE CREAM CONTAINS NON MILK FAT

Hand Made at
THE ROYAL OAK INN, GT. WISHFORD, SALISBURY, WILTS.

Hand Made
Chocolate Mint Crisps

Home made by 'Katie' at the
ROYAL OAK INN, GREAT WISHFORD
Tel. Salisbury 790229

Salisbury had, and still has, an excellent catering college and we employed several up and coming chefs from there. One was a young man named Stephen. He was a brilliant cook and a real character. He was also gay. Everyone loved Stephen, particularly the girls who worked with him. The pub kitchen had a large window overlooking the car park, and often one of the girls would remark that a hunk of a male was about to come into the pub. This was usually quickly followed by Stephen crying out,

"I saw him first," much to everyone's amusement.

He loved to go into the bars to meet the customers, discuss the food and proudly announce that he had prepared their meal. Stephen went on to be a chef in one of the top hotels in Brighton.

THIS WAS NOT PLANNED

In 1984 we were invited to a presentation by a training manager from our landlord, a brewery.

The theme was how to run a successful business. We duly attended. The following day one of the directors telephoned to enquire what we thought of this presentation.

"It was rubbish," I told him. "He had obviously never actually run a pub!"

"Oh dear," was his reply. "Maybe you would like to present to a group of prospective tenants?"

"No thanks, I'm too busy." I replied. But I did!

This presentation was to thirty prospective licensees and the subject was 'A Day In The Life of a Busy Publican'.

Presumably this was a success, as a few weeks later, Kate and I were approached by the senior training manager at the brewery. He was responsible for organising the training syllabus for their two week residential brewers society training course held at Donhead House, in Wiltshire.

At that time, The Brewers Society (an association of major breweries who owned their own pubs, tied to their beers), had established two week comprehensive training courses for people applying for tenancies of their pubs. One course was held in the midlands and the other in Wiltshire. It was held in the beautiful old Donhead House, a grade 11 listed building. The courses encompassed most aspects of running a pub including working on a real bar. The candidates were monitored carefully and the pass rate was about fifty percent. In those days, there were many applicants for each vacancy, meaning that the brewers could be choosy. Later, when The Beer Orders (explained later) changed the dynamics of the industry, applicants became scarce!

"We would like you both to lecture prospective tenants on 'Catering for Profit' based upon your experience at The Royal Oak.' He announced.

"No thanks, we are too busy." I replied. We did it anyway.

This was a whole new chapter in our career. In order to teach others we needed to ensure that every aspect of the subject was correct on the assumption that there would always be a bright spark in the audience to trip you up. Therefore, we swotted up on health and hygiene regulations, what bugs caused illness from poorly controlled kitchens, employment law etc.

Slides were made of each stage of preparation of meals through to service. We took photographs of our kitchens just before starting a session, during preparation and the chaotic state of the kitchens when the session had ceased. Menu planning, costing a meal, presentation and seasonal use of ingredients were discussed, in detail.

We thought that our first lecture went well. Afterwards, Geoff, the training manager, had a long list of suggestions for us. He had gently pointed out changes that he wanted, in a firm but totally professional manner. Geoff attended the courses, carefully observing the attendees to assess their suitability. Apart from lectures, when candidates worked sessions on the real bar, the way they conducted themselves was seriously taken into consideration. Geoff had an amazing gift of advising a candidate that they had failed in such a manner that it wasn't until a bit later that they realised. He would say

"You were really great, well done. Unfortunately you didn't pass, goodbye."

We continued training at the college twice a month until the courses ended a few years later.

ACCOUNTANTS?

Before we moved into The Oak we were advised to hire an accountant. The local Licensed Victuallers Association (LVA), suggested Moore Stephens Accountants based in Salisbury. We met the senior partner at the time, Graham Tate, who became our accountant, and a real friend throughout the rest of our time at "The Oak." He also played an important part in what followed.

We had mentioned our involvement in training prospective licensees at Donhead and one day, Graham asked if he could sit in on our presentation. A few weeks later he visited us and told us that, where possible, Moore Stephens preferred to have accountants who specialised in subjects such as farming, chemists etc.. This gave clients a much better service as their accountant understood the financial circumstances relating to their business. He said that they would like to add the licensed trade to their portfolio and asked if we would be interested in helping them. The logic was, that although they, as accountants, were able to produce accounts for tax purposes, they were not able to advise on net or gross profit margins relevant to region or style of operation or overheads specific to our industry. Moore Stephens already had a large number of clients in the licensed trade (hence us being recommended to use them as our accountants), but quite a few were struggling financially. My role would be to interrogate the accounts of clients, investigate in detail how they managed their business, and suggest ways to improve the profitability. On this basis, I worked with Moore Stephens accountants on odd occasions while still running The Oak, and although I quite enjoyed it, only regarded it as an interesting sideline. Then changes within the brewery sector started.

THE DEMISE OF A LARGE NUMBER OF GOOD PUB OPERATORS

Ushers Brewery had a trading agreement with Watney Mann, hence us stocking their "Red Barrel" Draught beer. In 1974, Watney Mann was merged with Grand Metropolitan Hotels. By the end of the 1980's, six national brewers dominated the market for beer in the UK. They were: Allied Breweries, Bass Charrington, Watney Mann, Courage, Scottish and Newcastle, and Whitbread. This caused concerns about lack of competition and resulted in legislation commonly known as the 'Beer Orders' being passed. This legislation limited the number of pubs that could be tied to a brewer to 2000. Larger brewers were required to allow a guest beer to be purchased from a brewer of choice, at free trade prices. The industry had caught wind of these imminent changes and responded by forming pub owning companies (Pubcos).These companies were not brewers, but formed trading agreements with a brewer, thus obtaining income from rents and discounts from the associate brewer.

Grand Metropolitan's version was the Inntrepreneur lease for their newly formed Inntrepreneur Pub Company. They had realised that currently they owned a large number of pubs, run as Tenancies. Many were not trading well and nearly all of their properties were in need of repair, through neglect. They devised a scheme that in return for some security of tenure and the benefit of assignability, they could divulge themselves of the repair burden. The result was the "Inntrepreneur 20 year lease". This was a Full Repairing and Insuring (FRI), but could be assigned after five year.

The logic was that currently, regardless of the level of trade, all a tenant received, when he/she left the pub, was the value of the fixtures, fittings, stock and glassware. However, equity could accrue if the business was successful, with an assignable lease. The lessees would still be tied to a brewer for beer with rent reviews (upward only), every five years. Also, providing the rent was paid on time, there was security of tenure for twenty years.

All of the Usher Pub estate, now owned by Grand Metropolitan Hotels, were to transfer to Inntrepreneur leases at their next rent review point, or prior, by negotiation. Our review point was March 1988. Our involvement in training at Donhead, had resulted in us becoming very friendly with many brewery personnel, some of whom were being transferred to the Inntrepreneur Pubco. Due to this relationship, I was able to attend presentations by Inntrepreneur's lawyers, where they outlined the terms of the lease to their new teams. They made it absolutely clear that the terms of their lease were "non negotiable!'

I was not impressed. Soon after, I was approached by two employees of the new company whose job was to agree terms for the new lease, with tenants. We were offered a new lease with a hike of 12,000 pounds on top of our current rent, with the added legal responsibility of repairing our dear old pub. They advised that we should take legal advice and obtain a structural survey of the building. They were slick negotiators, emphasizing that our business would eventually realise a good premium due to its profitability, under this new scheme.

We had reached a crossroads in our career as licensees. Kate was often heard to say that she was spending her whole life in the kitchen and, apart from not having bars on the window, she might as well be in prison. I, on the other hand, had started to visit pubs on behalf of Moore Stephens and was beginning to see life outside of The Oak. We discussed the situation with Graham, our accountant, and his advice was that we would be stupid to sign the new lease. He actually told me to examine our situation as if I was working for Moore Stephens and then make some considered decisions. I took his advice and reluctantly came to the conclusion that with initial hike in rent, further rent increases every five years and the repair liability, the financial implications were not good.

Graham suggested that I could become a partner in the Salisbury office of Moore Stephens, subject to head office approval. I jokingly remarked that when we first arrived at The Oak, aged twenty three, I was very fit and had said,

"There is no one in this bar that I couldn't evict if I had to." However, having been at the Pub for twenty two years, I had to rephrase this to,

"I'm not sure if there is anyone in this bar that I could evict."

We decided *not* to sign the lease, and to leave our business and home of twenty-two years. Running a very successful business and living on the job had become totally consuming, and to break away from this was scary. Our lovely bungalow in north Wales was to become home. Kate had always wanted to go to university, so applied to Bangor University as a mature student to study English and History. She was accepted and eventually obtained a BA Hons.

I went to London with Graham Tate, met the senior partner of Moore Stephens head office and subsequently became a partner in the Salisbury office.

Then came the dreaded day to leave The Royal Oak. I had started working with a well known pub valuer as part of my training for my new role. One of the major expenses a prospective licensee has, on top of an advance in rent, is the value of fixtures, fittings, stock and glassware. Therefore I needed to be able to undertake these valuations in order to offer considered advice. With this knowledge we were able to conduct our own valuation plus in our case, goodwill, when we finally left The Royal Oak, thanks to our inside knowledge!

BEHIND LOTS OF BARS

Undoubtedly, the Inntrepreneur Lease was the forerunner in changing the structure of pub tenures for many years. Unfortunately, it had been constructed with the objective of enhancing the capital value of their estate, by incorporating large hikes in rents and relinquishing their repair liability while retaining discounts from a brewer. They used the incentive of security of tenure coupled with the opportunity of profitably assigning a successful business to convince existing tenants to sign their lease and to woo prospective entrepreneurs.

This radical change in approach using a cold, unemotional, purely commercial objective, in my opinion, was largely responsible for ripping the soul out of a large section of the licensed trade in Britain. This caused the financial downfall of many good licensees. Many were very good charismatic operators but unused to the sudden responsibility of coping with an FRI lease.

Major banks were enticed to participate and offer loans to new licensees. We became involved with Lloyds who initially embraced the perceived opportunity. After the failure of most of the businesses that they had loans with, their interest ceased suddenly.

Corporate greed had now entered the pub industry! Fortunately, many regional brewers did not, and have not, succumbed to this strategy or become absorbed into the conglomerates. Most retain conventional tenancy agreements and some have evolved their own user friendly lease agreements as well. Many existing licensees did sign the Inntrepreneur lease without professional advice, and failed. Some 300 legal actions were taken against Inntrepreneur Pub. Co, which speaks for itself. Other brewers and Pub co's followed with their own leases, but all made radical improvements to the Inntrepreneur version!

BASIC TRAINING (AGAIN!)

During my first year with Moore Stephens, it was necessary to really understand what kind of people went into the licensed trade either as tenants, lessees or purchasers of a freehold pub. We placed an advertisement in The Morning Advertiser, the recognised conduit of information for prospective or existing licensees, suggesting that anyone contemplating the licensed trade as a career would benefit from talking to us first. This caused some reaction from licensed trade selling agents and brokers who interpreted this as a threat to their services. It was!! However, we persevered and for a fee of fifty pounds I discussed and advised many aspiring licensees. Quite a few decided not to proceed once they became aware of the commitment both physically and financially.

MOORE STEPHENS
CHARTERED ACCOUNTANTS

A SPECIALISED ACCOUNTANCY SERVICE TO THE LICENSED TRADE

The Business Support Service

MOORE STEPHENS BUSINESS SUPPORT SYSTEM

What is it?

A simple, modern, efficient, **accountancy system** requiring minimum input from the licensee. It provides prompt, accurate information.

The success of your business could depend on it.

What is your involvement?

Simply complete a straight forward weekly cash sheet and promptly return it to us.

What do you receive from us?

A full explanatory meeting with specialist personnel is arranged to discuss your requirements. From the following range of services a package *can* be structured to suit *your* business.

1. A monthly report showing actual versus breakeven performance is sent to you with appropriate advice where necessary.
2. Quarterly management accounts will be sent to you within 4 weeks of the quarters end and they are presented in a simple and understandable format.
3. Draft annual accounts to Inland Revenue requirements are presented to you within 6 weeks of your financial year end.
4. Quarterly wet and dry extended stocktaking can be arranged according to your requirements. A monthly service if required is available.
5. Preparation of quarterly VAT returns.
6. PAYE administration can be supplied according to your staffing levels.
7. Direct access to your personal accounts manager.
8. An annual accounts review at your premises with a Moore Stephens Chartered Accountant.

What are the benefits to you?

1. You are not swamped with unnecessary paperwork and information – our system only provides you with simple and accurate facts thus leaving you free to concentrate on what you do best – running your business.
2. The system is controlled at all stages by Moore Stephens Chartered Accountants together with specialist consultants, who are all dedicated to supporting your business. You can feel confident that your best interests will be served when you use Moore Stephens services to the Licensed Trade.
3. As an option – a meeting can be arranged to review your business at your premises by a Moore Stephens Senior Consultant – and our fees would be charged at cost.

◆

Our aim is to create an Accountancy/Business Monitoring System, to suit your business and your budget.

Our initial consultation is free.

Call now for further details of this and any of our other services.

Please keep this card for future reference.

MOORE STEPHENS
Licensed Trade Division
can also provide the following services:

Freehold and Leasehold Sales and Acquisitions
at competitive fee rates.

Lease and Rent Negotiations
we have successfully carried out many
such negotiations on behalf of clients.

Licensed Trade Insurance
a package designed specifically for your
business in conjunction with Sun Alliance.

Finance
we can assist in arranging a personal
introduction to a suitable source with
supporting information as required

I continued to work with a reputable licensed trade valuer who taught me the fundamentals of valuing inventories in detail. We compared values on many occasions until he felt confident that I had the knowledge to go it alone. I was then able to value inventories on behalf of our clients when they were moving into a pub. The outgoing tenant or lessee had their own valuer and both valuers compared notes and agreed, or disagreed, on the final amount. The fee was a percentage of the agreed value.

This valuation knowledge came in handy when we were acting for a couple moving into an Inntrepreneur leased pub in Devon. They had been advised that the ingoing amount consisted of a proportion of rent plus the value of the inventory. We were to act as accountants and advisers. I attended on the day that they moved in. When I was advised of the amount being charged for the inventory, I had a good look over the whole property. The value suggested bore no resemblance to the true value of the fixtures and fittings. Carpets were threadbare, curtains were in shreds and the furniture was unfit for purpose!. I reckoned that the true value was less than half that being charged.I also knew the logic behind the amount suggested. The outgoing lessees were in arrears with their rent and the value suggested for the ingoing inventory was to 'balance the books'. *Not* by my clients! I was quickly on the telephone to my contacts at Inntrepreneur in Bristol. I explained the situation and advised them that our clients would not move into the pub unless my valuation of the inventory, which was fair, was accepted. I added that I was quite prepared to have my valuation scrutinised. They accepted and we retained very happy clients.

I became a respected thorn in the side of Inntrepreneur, and most of the other PubCos, for some time.

NOT ON MY MANOR!

We had been engaged as accountants by a young gay couple who were taking on a large Pub in London, also on an Inntrepreneur lease. They were shrewd operators who had been very professional. In their research and financial projections for their new project and knew the location of the pub well. Although the rent was very high, so were their projected profit margins. When I commented that their prices seemed on the high side, one of them commented,

"When two young boys are looking lovingly at each other, the last thing on their minds is the cost of the drink!"

However, not long after they moved into the pub one of them telephoned to say that they had been approached by heavies demanding 400 pounds a week protection money. Could we advise?

A few weeks earlier, Kate and I had been to London to meet Nick, our son. We had arranged to meet for lunch in a large pub. At the door of the pub were two very large, extremely well dressed doormen. For some reason, I can't remember why, they were only allowing couples to enter. I told them that we were meeting our son, who they would easily recognise as he was on crutches, and could they let him in. They were fine with this. I was impressed with their professionalism and asked if they had a business card. They produced an equally impressive card, which simply stated, 'Problems Sorted!' and a contact number.

Back in the office, I found this card and called the main man. I explained the situation regarding protection money in London and asked him if he could help.

"I am in Salisbury next week, I'll call in for a chat," he said.

A mountain of a man duly arrived a week later. He was a very softly spoken, intimidating giant of a man, but a fascinating character. He said that he had recently had a team on the cross channel ferries. They had been called in by the shipping company because drug dealers were becoming a nuisanse on their boats.

"How did you deal with that?" I asked him.

"Well, we advised the police that we were involved, and six of us went on the ferry. The dealers, all youngsters, tended to work in the bar area. We identified them quite easily and quietly surrounded them. I asked the leader if he knew how far we were from Dover."

"Why?" he replied.

"Because that's how far you and your chums will swim if we catch you here ever again," I advised him. "Here is my card, give it to whoever pulls your strings, and tell him we don't jest."

I explained to him that my clients in London were experiencing problems concerning protection threats.

"I wondered if you could help them?" I asked him.

"Leave it to me, I'll soon sort that out. "He replied very confidently. I know that pub well. It will cost your guys 500 pounds and they will not be bothered again."

"How do I know that will be the case."? I asked, being a suspicious sort of bloke.

He gave me a withering look, so I kept quiet.

He visited the boys in London, they paid him the money and they did not receive protection threats again.

I called my problem solving giant and thanked him.

"What did you do?" I asked him.

"I know the gang involved and their head man." He advised.

"So what did you say to him?" I enquired with interest.
"I just said '*not* on *my* manor.' He got the message." He chuckled.

This was an interesting experience of a world I knew little about, or wished to.

JOHN AND GREENALLS

It soon became obvious that I couldn't manage the licensed trade unit alone. Graham Tate and his accountant partners covered the appropriate accounting side but I was travelling up and down the country visiting licensees in trouble one day, valuing inventories another day and helping prospective licensees on a one to one basis in the office in between.

John Pownall had been a senior manager with Grand Metropolitan Hotels. When they formed Inntrepreneur, John's department had been disbanded. We had met during our stints at Donhead training college and had become good friends. John had valuable contacts at a high level within the industry and joined me in 1990.

We were expanding our client base gradually but not quickly enough at that stage to convince partners, other than Graham, that it was ever likely to become a major income stream.

Fortunately, John knew the MD of Greenalls Inns.

Greenall Inns was a brewing company situated in Warrington, Cheshire. Their estate consisted of over 1500 pubs. About 600 were operated on a simple franchise scheme which included Greenalls providing them with basic accounting services. These were outsourced to a local firm of accountants. This really gave them knowledge of the financial health of their estate but did not offer any real support. We saw an opportunity for our company and John organised a meeting with their MD and finance director.

We outlined exactly how we operated, produced samples of our management accounts and advised on the cost to Greenalls. The MD considered our proposal then announced that our fees were twice what he expected to pay, and without another word, stood up and left the meeting.

Exactly one year later, we were called back to Greenalls, this time to meet just with the Finance Director. He showed us a map of the country with over 30 names of accounting firms marked upon it.

"I have talked to representatives from each of these accounting firms," he said, "and none could match the service or fee structure that you guys presented to us last year, so if you still want to take on the accounting service for our estate, you can."

It took nearly a year to transfer nearly six hundred accounts over to Moore Stephens and involved opening an office in Altrincham nr. Manchester, then recruiting more staff. Greenalls had employed several staff within their company to manage their accounting service as well as those contracting out. Several of the Greenall staff transferred to our new Altrincham office team, but the removal of clients from the firm of accountants involved me and one of our senior accountants visiting their offices on several occasions. To say that we received a frosty reception, is an understatement!

We expanded quite rapidly, due to this contract, and soon realised that our service with management accounts backed by people with specific knowledge of the licensed trade, had enormous potential. John and I developed our 'Business Support Pack'. Each customer was provided with a folder containing an example set of Management Accounts depicting suggested overhead costs against budget, gross and net profit margins, together with a sample of a Balance Sheet.

Also enclosed were menu and drink costing sheets. We organised regular stock checks from reputable stock takers, as these were integral to providing accurate information.

We also decided on a fixed price accounting service based on turnover. It was subject to us receiving relevant information as required regularly, on time. This was a move away from the conventional fee system used by the accounting proffesion, where clients are charged an hourly rate. This fixed price arrangement certainly caused some alarm within our Chartered Accountant partners.

OVER TRADING?

While we were taking on new customers based upon licensees from independent brewers, Inntrepreneur, and Greenalls, an employee from Scottish and Newcastle brewery contacted me to arrange a meeting. She met me at Southampton Airport. She was armed with all of the literature that Greenalls supplied to prospective franchisees! Apparently, her brief was to try and put together a cross between a managed house operation and a tenancy. Knowing our involvement in other Pub Co's, in particular, their franchise agreements, she hoped that we could help.

Client confidentiality was important but we endeavoured to steer her towards a basic franchise system. She didn't think this fitted her brief and despite her efforts, unfortunately she did not present a satisfactory proposal to her peers, so true to the Scottish and Newcastle philosophy, which was,

"If you didn't succeed you had failed."

Consequently, she left the company.

During this process, however, I had become quite involved with several senior members of the Scottish and Newcastle team. They could not be regarded as 'friends' but we had a formidable formal respect for each other which enabled us to work towards a mutually satisfactory outcome. After advising them of the benefits, they eventually decided on a franchise arrangement for their tied estate. The good news for us was that because of our successful involvement with the Greenalls franchise, their version was to include the provision of accounting services. Not willing to put all their eggs in one basket and believing that competition resulted in better service and keener pricing, they engaged another firm of accountants as well. So, in conjunction with this other firm of accountants, we had now landed another large contract.

However, prior to commencing this contract I had to give a presentation to the Scottish and Newcastle board of Directors in Edinburgh. The date and venue of this presentation was announced with only two days' notice whileI was on holiday with Kate, in Cornwall.

I advised the Director from Scottish and Newcastle that I was on holiday and couldn't make it at such short notice.

His retort was,

"If you want the contract, be there," and terminated the call.

Despite flights from Plymouth to Edinburgh being few and far between, I was there!

The presentation was to outline exactly how we would manage this contract and what resources we had. I quoted from the Moore Stephens national brochure which indicated that the company had offices throughout the UK as well as offices in the Capital of countries worldwide! It also depicted a turnover of millions of pounds. I then used a powerpoint presentation to outline the accounting process with examples of what a franchisee would actually receive.

Graham Tate, the senior partner of Moore Stephens, Salisbury, attended this presentation with me and his reaction afterwards was.

"Bloody hell Colin, that was very impressive, but related to Moore Stephens as a National and International firm of chartered accountants, not your little outfit. You do not have the staff, the offices or the equipment to cope with this! You need help and quick." he added, with exasperation.

Moore Stephens were concerned that this was a precarious situation as we were 'over trading'. They introduced us to Compass Connections, a London based company with offices in Mumbai. Compass employed qualified accountants in Mumbai and provided outsourcing services worldwide.

They were amazing, and to everyone's relief, soon acquainted themselves with the situation.

To cope with the ongoing huge increase in our client base we opened offices in Newcastle, Leicester, and Edinburgh. We employed junior trainee accountants as account managers, each responsible for twenty customers . They operated on a regional basis, reporting to a senior manager in each office. We realised the importance of staff being local to the client in view of the disparity of dialects throughout the Country. I trained them in the basics of running a pub including visits to kitchens and pub cellars, plus presentations. We provided simple cash sheets that licensees completed weekly. These were emailed to their relevant account manager. The process was; The cash sheets were emailed by the licensee to their local accounts manager, but in fact went straight to India. There they were coded, management accounts produced, and emailed to the relevant real regional account manager in England or Scotland. They were checked and relayed to the customer. Due to the time difference in India, the turnaround of information was impressively swift. Our staff, in the UK and their respective operators in India, were in regular contact, but neither the customers, or Scottish and Newcastle personnel initially, knew of the Mumbai connection! However, as the contract grew, it did become imperative to involve the Scottish and Newcastle team.

Their initial reaction was unprintable. They insisted that our finance director accompany one of their team dedicated to the franchise scheme, to Mumbai. Fortunately, they were hugely impressed, and later members from our team in India visited them in Scotland. This continued to be a huge contract and eventually even involved a number of Scottish and Newcastle managed houses having all of their accounting services contracted to us. The licensees, however, only ever had contact with their account manager in the UK. They were never informed of the Indian involvement.

GOODBYE GREENALLS

In 1999, Greenalls Inns was acquired by Nomura- a Japanese Bank. Greenalls franchise scheme had already been nominated in a national competition for franchise schemes. The finals were held at the Grosvenor Hotel, in London. I was invited to attend with the team from Nomura, who were now in control.

I was seated next to one of their directors. He informed me that he had examined several sets of accounts that had been prepared by us and it was obvious to him that turnover was being understated in most cases and the businesses were not declaring their true profitability.

This really annoyed me and I replied.

"I have visited many of these licensees and can assure you that you are miss informed as many are struggling to survive."

"Why don't you come with me to visit a few of the pubs that Nomura have acquired and see first hand?"

"Never,"he replied. "We do not want to get personally involved" "This is purely a business transaction."

This confirmed my conclusion that the industry that I loved and had an affinity with my fellow licensees, had been identified as being ripe for financial speculation, with little or no consideration for the people it affected.

Nomura then acquired Inntrepreneur!

We continued to provide accountancy services as usual to ex Greenall customers as their franchises remained in place.

One of Greenall's franchisees that we provided accounting services for was Liz Dawn, the memorable actress who played Vera Duckworth in the Coronation Street series. She was a real character and her pub was The Old Grapes, in Manchester. It was situated close to the old Granada film studios, and the cast of Coronation Street, and many other actors used it as their regular watering hole. There was a roped-off area reserved for the actors. The walls were adorned with dozens of photos of actors and Liz was identifying them to me. We came to a picture of Paul O'Grady, who became famous as a drag artist with his Lily Savage character. His photo was positioned alongside one of Lily.

"Do you know, Vera?" I confessed. "For ages I thought that Lily Savage really was a woman."

She looked at me in amazement, slapped me soundly on the back, and in her mancunian accent said, "My word love, you really have led a sheltered life!" Other photos included Cilla Black, a great friend of Paul.

PARTNERS!

Whitbread then formed their Pub Partnership division in 1992 and Courage soon followed with their version of a franchise agreement. Accountancy services were not mandatory in these agreements, but due to our reputation, many franchisees became clients.

I visited a Whitbread pub situated close to the river severn near Gloucester. The license who was an American was disillusioned by the discrepancy regarding the price that he paid for beer supplied by Whitbread brewery compared to the price that his pal running a Free House opposite, paid for beer brewed by the same company. To add insult to injury, their beer was actually delivered on the same dray wagon. I remember being with him on one occasion and he looked across as beer was being delivered to the Free house opposite.

"Pub Partners, be damned," He said bitterly." Where I come from, that kind of partner would end up with lead boots at the bottom of the Potomac!"

I visited another Whitbread pub, also run by an American couple, later the same day. They were quite old with no previous trade experience. They had only been in the pub for two weeks and were trying to operate a simple food service from a kitchen situated one floor down from the bar, which meant carrying trays of food up and down a flight of stairs. This was proving to be physically challenging for the Licensee's wife, who was the cook. I asked them who had interviewed them from Whitbread and who had suggested this particular pub.

"A young manager who reckoned this pub was ideal for us and easy to manage." was the answer.

I was friendly with the senior district manager at Whitbread and called him to express my dismay at this situation. He was quite sympathetic and agreed that in hindsight that pub did not suit that couple.

"The problem that we have is there are just so few applicants for our pubs at the moment and our young managers are tasked to lease them ,to keep our income stream flowing," he explained. Just fifteen years earlier, when we had been lecturing at Donhead college, couples were queuing to enter the trade. By the mid nineties the average time a couple stayed in a pub was less than two years!

NIGHT CLUBS

Licensees operating nightclubs fascinated me. Invariably they were likeable rogues but great characters. I visited one in the Reading area to try to interest him in our accounting package.

He was a healthy looking young man aged about thirty. The club was large, and had a number of rooms on the first floor that the licensee rented to students. The licensee lived elsewhere, but a manager lived in.

I went through our package with him, over coffee, and he listened intently. When I had finished my sales pitch, he grinned and said, "Interesting mate, but we couldn't use you, you are too honest for us!"

"Tell me more." I answered inquisitively.

"I'm not giving all of our secrets away but occasionally, our little headcount clicker seems to stick and we have a few more customers in the club than we are licensed for which means that the door takings need a little tweak to make our records legal, if you get my meaning?" He remarked with a grin.

We did however get on well together and he retained us on a consultancy basis. He was having a dispute with his Pub Co over their supply agreement. He was tied to Courage for beers and was being accused of purchasing outside of his tie, which he was!

I advised him that we would investigate. While I was talking to him outside, suddenly a suit case followed by clothes, books and a chair came whizzing past us to land on the pavement.

"What the hell is going on?" I asked.

"Some student hasnt paid his rent," he chuckled. "You know in our business they say 'no pay, no dray' while we say 'no rent, you're out'."

"The students are probably safer staying here than in most of the seedy digs in town, so that guy's room will be re-let today, I'll bet"."

We resolved the supply issue using some compromise. He was definitely buying outside of his supply agreement, but we identified that he was actually buying considerably more beer from his nominated supplier than any lessee had in the past, in that club. The dispute was dropped.

THE MAGIC MIRROR

Another club that we did actually act for as accountants, was probably even more dodgy, but the licensee was a great character. He always made me very welcome and he ran a tight ship.

Again, he was big and physically in shape. Everywhere he went outside of the club though, he was accompanied by two heavies as protection. In my opinion this was more for show than anything else, but we were not sure what other pies he had his fingers in, in town.

When the club was operating, he employed a number of security staff situated strategically throughout the premises, not just at the entrance. He regularly worked on the entrance as well as he was convinced that he could spot potential trouble better than most. The security team had a very sophisticated communication system. Each security staff member was fitted with a headset and had a fixed location in the club. They were in constant communication with each other and could move quickly to any part of the club to sort out any trouble. They even had a security member situated in each toilet block as the sinks had occasionally been used as urinals.

In each toilet, above each sink was a mirror with a sign saying, 'This is a magic mirror. Piss in the sink and you will wake up outside.'

I'm sure that a few customers had tested that, to their regret!

I'M ON YOUR SIDE!

It's not easy when you visit a licensee who is not doing well financially to point out the problem, particularly if it is him. My regular introduction under those circumstances was,

"Believe me, I am totally on your side but you may not like what I tell you."

For instance how can you be polite when you have been called in to help someone running a big town house in Bristol when confronted with the licensee, gut hanging over his belt, in a singlet, sweat from both armpits, and reeking of booze.

"Look in the mirror, chum, and you'll see the problem," is the obvious remark.

However, diplomacy works better, especially when he is considerably bigger than you. I realised that some pubs in certain areas needed a big, tough looking bloke to be successful as he would be dealing with an equally tough set of customers.

Often, the licensee in such establishments had started drinking heavily as well, and had become more of a drinking mate with his customers to the detriment of running a successful business.

My experience of being at The Royal Oak for a long time usually resulted in licensees accepting me as 'one of them', and when I gently pointed out that their situation was likely to not only make them bankrupt but kill them, generally they listened. I sometimes remember advising a licensee that he would probably make more money and be happier, stocking shelves in Tesco.

"What should we do then?" was the usual question (I've edited this considerably, as the language to reach this point was usually loaded with expletives!)

"Buck up, or get out while you still have some dignity," was my response.

Quite often the latter was the agreed outcome, and I would help negotiate a realistic exit plan with their brewer or pub co. This was not always easy as these situations made letting the pub even more difficult for the brewer or Pub Co. On another occasion, also in Bristol, when I tried to gently explain that the licensee was the problem, he picked me up and threw me out! Bastard!

ALSO NEAR BRISTOL

Another visit that went wrong was when I visited a pub that was situated right alongside the river.. The licensees had only recently moved in and were struggling financially This wasn't an easy fix as trade had originally mostly come from boats tying up alongside from visiting merchant vessels. The licensee informed me that research had informed them that the pub was very profitable many years ago when the sailors used it as a brothel. I mused over this and jokingly remarked that perhaps we should investigate this approach again.

"*Not* funny, get out." was the reply.

You can't win 'em all!

SELL FOOD - MAKE MONEY?

An extremely large pub in Leicester was being operated by a young couple who had developed a huge catering operation with live entertainment most weekends. Their turnover was huge, but their profitability was not.

I was, and still am, amazed that people running food operations invariably base their selling prices on similar outlets rather than proper costing. This was such a case. I spent some time helping them use our costing sheets (Such costing programmes are online now!) The result was that they were selling several thousand meals per week but averaging a loss of just under twenty pence per meal. They had also fallen into the trap of always using the same ingredients and not taking into account seasonal price rises and adjusting accordingly. Basic catering procedures. They were a lovely couple and we became good friends.

NO FOOD - MAKE MONEY?

I visited a big pub in a fairly rough area of Bristol and the licensee informed me that the health inspector had forced his food operation to close due to the facilities not being adequate. He had been operating from the domestic kitchen, and frankly, I agreed with the health inspector!

"Let's try something that works in a Pub in Birmingham", I suggested. "Situated close to you, is an Indian restaurant and a Chinese restaurant and both do take away meals.

"Do a deal with them and open an account," I advised."

You display their menus in the pub, the customer places their order with you, pays you, and you phone the order to the restaurant and they deliver."

"The good news is that you do not need any catering equipment as you are not preparing any food. The customer purchases a disposable knife, fork and plate, when they order their food as part of the deal. When they have finished eating, all you need is a rubbish bag for the debris!"

I visited again a few weeks later and he had embraced the idea and was very grateful. A happy customer.

WHO NEEDS TRAINING?

I was called in to advise a couple who had purchased a small, upmarket hotel in the midlands. Although they were reasonably booked with guests staying at the hotel, they were not making any money.

Once again the catering operation had not been costed properly. No costing for each dish on the menu had been made. Profit margins for drinks were equally not controlled. They had a comprehensive wine list but announced that most of the wines sold were in the cheaper bracket.

I explained that to sell the more expensive wines it was necessary to work on a profit per bottle rather than stick to a percentage across the wine list.

We spent a whole day addressing the situation. It transpired, that before purchasing the hotel, the owner had been a dentist

"How long did you train to become a dentist?" I asked him.

"Five years," he replied.

"And how long did you train to become a hotelier?" I said.

"Message received" he said grimly. They sold the hotel soon after.

TAX. NO THANKS!

One lovely couple, a mother and daughter, were running a pub, off the beaten track in Wiltshire. They had a really good food trade and were imaginative with the names of their dishes. They specialised in fish dishes, one being called "Cod Almighty"

While examining their accounts I noticed that no income had been included for Bed and Breakfast sales. I asked one of the local customers if the pub had people staying for B&B.

"Crumbs, yes, they are very busy with guests and they rave about the breakfast that Molly serves them,"he told me.

"Molly, you forgot to record your Bed and Breakfast income." I told her.

"No I b--y well did not, "she said. "I'm not getting up at the crack of dawn and working myself to death to give my hard earned cash to the tax man." she replied indignantly.

"It might be an idea to remove the sign at the end of the road and the one outside of the pub offering, 'Bed and the best Breakfast in England', Molly. They are a bit of a giveaway, I reckon." I replied with a chuckle.

My job was to help her business to succeed and that did not involve a tax investigation.

I think that she recorded some income from B&B from then, but certainly not all!

A similar situation that was a gift to the tax man looking for undeclared income, was when I visited a huge boozer in Manchester. It was close to a major football ground and catered specifically for people visiting matches. Beer was sold in plastic pint glasses, on trays of six at a time. They also had about ten fruit machines!

Income declared from machine income was minimal.

"Fred, do you realise that the company providing those fruit machines, declares their income *and* your share, to the taxman. Your brewer also gets a slice of the income?"

Amazingly, from then all income from fruit machines was declared but beer sales seemed to drop!!

Trading as Moore Stephens Licensed Trade accountants Ltd, had enabled the company to bid and obtain decent sized contracts, but this success had not been anticipated by the London Head Office whose core business was definitely not pubs. They did not want to be labelled 'Pub Accountants'!

Chantry Vellacott, another national firm of accountants, had become interested in acquiring us. They purchased Moore Stephens shares and became the major shareholders. This new relationship worked well, as although our team of accountants had grown to match the expanding client base, we still didn't have any trained *tax* accountants, essential for year end tax returns, directly employed by our Licensed trade division. Tax had been dealt with by an internal arrangement with Moore Stephen, but was more suited to Chantrey Vellacott's office locations.

We now changed our trading name from Moore Stephens Licensed Trade Accountants (MSLTA Ltd.) to MSLTA Ltd. Trading as MILESTONE Accountants and John joined me as joint Managing Director.

In 2005, we had offices in Edinburgh, Manchester, Leicester, Newcastle and three in Salisbury, one being dedicated to producing payroll services. Not long after this association, Chantry Vellacott, in anticipation of John and I retiring, appointed a senior manager as our successor.

The number of pubs in England had reduced from 75000 in 1969 to about 50000 in 2005. We had experienced a situation where people were keen to take a pub, to a situation where there was a dearth of applicants. In 1988 I was discussing this situation with the MD of a regional brewer in the North. I asked him what criteria he expected from a prospective tenant.

"Colin, if they have the cash and can lift the latch to get in, I'll accept them, the situation is that dire," he replied sadly.

Fortunately about 20,000 pubs remained, and still remain, with regional brewers, who offer conventional tenancy arrangements and in some cases, acceptable lease agreements as well.

THE BEERAGE

These regional brewers, often family businesses that had been in the family for generations, were fondly referred to as 'The Beerage'. One of these is Shepherd Neame, situated In Faversham, Kent, England, founded in 1864. Their beers were, and still are, one of my favorites. One beer is called 'SPITFIRE'. It was first brewed in 1960 to commemorate the battle Britain fought over the skies of Kent, many years before. Many amusing beer mats are associated with it, including 'Joy Stick', 'Beware of Enemy Infiltration', and the famous, 'No Fokker Comes Close.'

Spitfire Beer Mat

The major pub co's have evolved in a very positive manner, offering training courses, and support. Many old boozers have disappeared and food is offered in the vast majority of pubs. It is generally recognised that as in any business, it is those that act professionally that survive.

STAPLEFORD 229

Wishford, Near

26th

M r & Mrs

DR. TO

The "Royal Oak"

D. C. GREENHOUSE - PROPRIET

5th–26th June.   B & B @ 13/6
                 Garage

Ultimately, I reckon that Kate and I had one of the first Gastro Pubs in England!

Original Receipt of a Lord and Lady on their wedding nig

IN HINDSIGHT - SOME RESEARCH!

In 1967, we didn't have a computer or access to the internet. Our adding machine had a handle that was pulled to add numbers and was the size of a small typewriter! Consequently, our information regarding the history of The Royal Oak was scanty and relied on local knowledge.

We now have access to the internet and with the help of Wiltshire and Swindon History Centre, have gleaned the following information.

In 1618, there was an Alehouse called 'The Tap', in the village of Great Wishford. Records that mention The Royal Oak date from 1822, but in some instances still refer to it as The Tap.

In 1841, there was a census and Frederick Shergold aged 25 and his wife Philadelphia, aged 20 were listed as 'Innkeepers'. (Coincidentally, they were of similar ages to us when we started at the Oak)

The Inn officially became The Royal Oak about 1861

The Shergolds raised four children. In 1871, one daughter was listed as a barmaid, and they had a servant, named Jane, aged 74! In 1881, another daughter, Pauline, married Charles Lucas and he was listed as the Innkeeper until 1891. In 1891, the Inn changed hands and Michael Petty became the Innkeeper with his wife. They raised six children while at The Oak.

Kelly's directory lists the following Innkeepers.
1889-1898 Michael Petty
1902 Mrs. Ann Petty
1907 Albert Fox
1911 William Malone

1918-1921 Joseph Gard
1923-1027 John Berry
(Also listed at this time was B&B, Lunches and teas)
1931 Lewis Hamblin
1935-1939 Reginald Musslewhite

The Royal Oak was purchased from the Pembroke Estate in 1920, by Ushers Brewery of Trowbridge, Wiltshire and included three acres, two rods and twenty three perches of land.

No major changes to the building were made from that time until we arrived. There had, however, been several outbuildings and additions to the pub over time, all of which, including a third chimney stack, had gone. What was called the Club Room when we arrived and converted into a restaurant was listed in the records as the Brew House.

We had been advised, not long after we moved into The Royal Oak, that the Pub was haunted, but in the twenty two years that we lived there and raised two children we only felt contented vibes. Apparently, folk that lived there afterwards didn't feel the same!

The pub had several licensees after us, but regrettably they were not successful. It was closed for a period but hopefully it is now thriving once again as a successful business. We wish the current licensee every success. We now live in New Zealand but would love to visit again one day.

Our 'Life Behind Bars' provided an abundance of special memories, some good, some not so good, some hilarious, some very sad. Just a few are shared above. There are lots more- some best forgotten! Many board meetings and negotiations with senior management in most major Pub Co's were involved in the later journey, but most don't make amusing reading!

Running a successful pub is mentally and physically demanding, but can be a very rewarding profession. Like many of our predecessors, Kate and I raised two children while at the pub. Both went to university. Nick is now a Consultant Cardiologist in New Zealand and Jacky manages one of the top forest nurseries in America.

John and I retired in 2005, and the company continued until 2008 when it was absorbed into another firm of accountants. John is able to pursue his love of golf and I manage a family vineyard and write children's books with Kate, in New Zealand.

Please visit theadventuresofcaptainstinkyandsailorpuss.com and mahanahills.co.nz

To Kate and all of the wonderful team who made The Oak such a great success, thank you.

Copyright 2024 COLIN FISHER
ISBN 9780995129559

All rights reserved. This book may not be reproduced in whole or in part in any form, or by Andy means, without express permission from the publisher.

Published by:
COLIN FISHER/BOOKS
Petra Way,
Nelson 7173
NEW ZEALAND

THAT'S ALL FOLKS

To Kate and all of the wonderful team who made The Oak such a great success, thank you.

Copyright 2024   COLIN FISHER
ISBN   9780995129559

All rights reserved. This book may not be reproduced in whole or in part in any form, or by any means, without express permission from the publisher.

PUBLISHED BY
COLIN FISHER/BOOKS
Petra Way,
Nelson 7173
NEW ZEALAND

www.ingramcontent.com/pod-product-compliance
Lightning Source LLC
Chambersburg PA
CBHW041503010526
44118CB00001B/4